"When you meet Eli Andrew Ramer, you won't know what hit you. Did you fall in love or have a psychotic break? He has gotten inside your DNA and won't take no for an answer. The adage 'thou art that' is truer than you wish. For despite your best efforts, you feel his heart beating in your chest. His eyes looking out your sockets. And you gasp in amazement: You have been met and seen!"

—RANDY LEE HIGGINS,
author of *Salvo, Beyond Nirbikalpa*

"Andrew Ramer has been seeing things that 'aren't there' since he was in the womb. If you see things too, you must read this book. You probably won't find that your visions are the same as his. But you'll learn something powerful from his openness. Ramer's message: Even when they are unsettling, they offer us not danger but revelation."

—JONATHAN LERNER,
author of *Performance Anxiety*

"From the time baby Andy was wrapped in a yellow blanket he lived a life not quite in sync with the world. His willingness to flow with what came has allowed us all to benefit from those experiences. In *Tales of an Urban Mystic* he offers us the whole story, providing recognition to those who have shared a similar journey, and inspiration to those struggling with the twists and turns of fate."

—OLUWO BRIAN OLÁNIPÈKUN MADIGAN,
author of *The Orisa: Vision Quests*

"Andrew Ramer takes us on his spectacular journey 'over the threshold between times and worlds' in *Tales of an Urban Mystic*. What permeates these multiple realities is Andrew's boundless love and quest for meaning. He not only describes how he has tapped into his own potential, but as he implores us throughout the book, how 'everyone . . . has a share in the transformation of human life upon this planet.'"

—STEVE STROIMAN,
author of *Moses in Manhattan*

"I love Andrew Ramer's *Tales of an Urban Mystic*. Eli, as he is now called as an elder of the tribe, shares stories of his interior life—things people don't usually share. Eli tells about the kinds of spiritual experiences I've always wanted to promote in my own work. We don't see enough of this in gay culture, though so many of us have such rich interior lives. I was impressed with the storytelling—very easy reading."

—TOBY JOHNSON,
author of *Gay Perspective*

"A work of luminous honesty, self-knowledge, and wisdom. Ramer is a writer who manages to combine—in all his many books—earnestness and levity, a keen awareness of life's joyous gifts and innumerable tragedies. Perhaps a prophet, certainly the author of luscious prose."

—STEVEN J. ZIPPERSTEIN,
author of *Philip Roth: Stung by Life*

"With humor and vulnerability, Andrew invites us into the terrain of his inner world—from the presence of a vanished twin to angelic visitations and moments of revelation sparked by bees, books, and subway rides. If you've ever longed for a story that makes space for your own truths, memories, and your shimmering path toward wholeness—this book is for you."

—SHERI HOSTETLER,
co-author of *So We and Our Children May Live*

"This poetic memoir is a song of invitation. To recall. To live. To dream. More than anything, it is an invitation to loosen the bounds of time and space that tether us. Andrew's words delight the senses, evoke the imagination, and free the spirit. And the ending holds an even deeper invitation: to know ourselves as 'Earth Healers,' and to act from this most expansive self."

—PATRICIA PLUDE,
author of *The Art of Radical Listening*

"Mystical dreams, angels, reincarnations, radical faeries, ancestral visitations, spirit guides . . . all pop in and out of Andrew Ramer's embodied, self-revelatory life story. *Tales of an Urban Mystic* is a captivating, heartfelt journey through the multidimensional life of a great writer and super cool human."

—ANNIE SPRINKLE,
author of *Assuming the Ecosexual Position: The Earth as Lover*

"Eli Andrew Ramer has had many identities over the years: storyteller, angel-whisperer, channeler, prophet, sage. Here, he stands before us na-ked—yet surrounded by the magical beings, synchronicities, and spirits who have been his guides since before he was born. In these tales, the mun-dane mingles with the supernatural, the painful with the profound. I can say with certainty that you have never read a memoir like it."

—JAY MICHAELSON,
author of *The Secret That is Not a Secret: Ten Heretical Tales*

"Lily Tomlin once pondered, 'Why is it when we talk to God we're said to be praying but when God talks to us we're schizophrenic?' Given his pen-chant for hearing voices, remembering places he'd never been, and having encounters with beings from other realities, Andrew Ramer wondered as a child if indeed he were crazy. Happily, he learned to channel his experi-ences in ways that allowed him to forge profound connections with kindred spirits. *Tales of an Urban Mystic* is a delicious exercise in life review, as Ra-mer introduces us to the people, places, realizations, and visitations that formed him and led him through his 'amazing journey to Now.'"

—DON SHEWEY,
author of *Daddy Lover God: A Sacred Intimate Journey*

"This book is an excellent example of how some of us reach a level of spirituality or understanding, yet not in the same way. Different journeys, without any reference points, other than showing up for life. I've known Eli Andrew Ramer for over three decades, and he's an extraordinary example of what spirituality actually represents."

—KAREN HAUGHEY,
author of *Angels: Guardians of the Light*

"Professor Ramer is of what Dolores Cannon hails as 'the First Wave,' the vanguard, the pioneers, the bellwether. And though he is from the prosaic side of the uterus, I am deeply honored to proclaim him brother. Indeed, brother-in-arms, as we fling open the doors to that ineffable effulgence that has been quietly knocking since before time was time."

—GAVIN GEOFFREY DILLARD,
author of *The Comfort of Stone*

"Eli Andrew Ramer has always been a visionary guide, weaving together deep spirituality, Jewish wisdom, and queer experience with rare grace. In *Tales of an Urban Mystic*, he opens his heart and his many lives to us, sharing his journey through the lands of faerie with candor, humor, and luminous insight. This memoir is a gift for anyone who has ever sought to reconcile their mystical experiences with their everyday lives, or their spiritual and sexual selves."

—MARK HORN,
author of *Tarot and the Gates of Light*

"Hineni! – "Here I am." "I contain multitudes." Echoing the words of Abraham and Walt Whitman, Ramer invites readers into his rich inner landscape. He's a maggid, a teller of stories, and his tales of wonder, visitation and travel across space and time illuminate what it's like to become those multitudes. His words are a gift and an offering. You, too, he reminds us, have this fullness, these possibilities, this holiness."

—SANDRA BUTLER,
author of *Leaving Home at 83*

Tales of an Urban Mystic

BOOKS BY ANDREW RAMER

From Wipf and Stock:

Ever After

Our Tribe Chanting

Two Hearts Dancing

Two Flutes Playing

Texting with Angels

Fragments of the Brooklyn Talmud

Deathless

Torah Told Different

Queering the Text

Revelations for a New Millennium

The Spiritual Dimensions of Healing Addictions and Further Dimensions of Healing Addictions (with Donna Cunningham)

And:

Ask Your Angels (with Alma Daniel and Timothy Wyllie)

Angel Answers

Space Duck

The Dream Gardener

Tales of an Urban Mystic

A Spiraling Memoir

by ANDREW RAMER

RESOURCE *Publications* · Eugene, Oregon

TALES OF AN URBAN MYSTIC
A Spiraling Memoir

Resource Publications
An Imprint of Wipf and Stock Publishers
199 W. 8th Ave., Suite 3
Eugene, OR 97401

www.wipfandstock.com

PAPERBACK ISBN: 979-8-3852-5873-4
HARDCOVER ISBN: 979-8-3852-5874-1
EBOOK ISBN: 979-8-3852-5875-8
VERSION NUMBER 12/05/25

For everyone named in these tales,
relatives, teachers, and friends,
in and out of physical bodies,
with gratitude and love.
And for you, dear readers,
on your own spiritual journey,
wishing you every blessing.

When a new child is born in the family, the ancestors gather above it and whisper among themselves: "Maybe this will be the one who will tell our stories and heal our lineage." *Angeles Arrien*

Contents

A Pathway to These Tales

SIGMUND FREUD WROTE THAT "anatomy is destiny." In my case – it's geography. I was born on March 24, 1951 in Elm/hurst, Queens, New York, across the street from an amusement park called Fairyland, and since March 21st, 2016 I live in Oak/land, California, up the street from an amusement park called Fairyland. The slash marks in Elm/hurst and Oak/land are deliberate. I'm a great lover of trees and the books that come from them! And that Queen and those Fairies are important too – as in gay boy / gay man, magical friends with wings, and the fairies in fairy tales, which I've loved since I was a little boy.

From as far back as age three I heard voices in my head, remembered places I'd never been to, had encounters with beings from other realities, awake and in my dreams, and liked to leave my body in spirit and fly around my room. Given the time and culture I was raised in, I never heard other people talking about experiences like that, and from their reactions when I did, I knew at an early age to never talk about mine, tried to stay in my body, and did my very best to stop the voices, with some success during the day but none when I was dreaming. So you can probably understand why for much of my life I've asked myself: "Am I a mystic – or – a mistake?"

About ten years ago my spiritual director used the word prophet to describe me. Stunned, I said to her: "Thank you. But can we call that the p-word, please?" If someone else had been visited by dead relatives, angels, and spent decades taking dictation from God the Mother, occasionally Father, and increasingly a God whose pronouns are It/Its, collected in an unpublished book called *God-Waves,* they might be comfortable owning the p-word. (For prophet, not pissing.) But not me, for much of my life!

At 74 I know that we all come into the world with different gifts and know that in other times and places mine would have been recognized by the elders, who would have taught me to develop them for the good of our village, our tribe, the world. My guides and angels have told me again and again that many of the people in psych wards and wandering the street talking to people (not on a wireless device) who aren't there, came into the world with the same gifts I did, but lacked the support and guidance that I had.

In the dance of my different gifts – I'm vision-impaired, have a learning disability, can't drive, or dribble or shoot a basketball, not that I ever wanted to, and I still have to count on my fingers and struggle to keep my checkbook balanced, not that anyone else I know still uses a paper checkbook – I know I'm a good writer, artist, teacher, friend – and if you're reading this book I imagine it's because you're aware of your own innate gifts and are looking for stories to corroborate them, so that you can nurture and use them, for the betterment of yourself and the world.

○

My father was born in the Bronx, New York, in 1923 to an Orthodox Jewish family, my mother was born in Brooklyn, New York in 1925 to an atheist Communist/Socialist Jewish family, and I learned very different things from each of them. In Dad's family God was never spoken of but was always in the background – of their prayers, blessings, and actions – ever-present like the water in a fishbowl is present for the fish. When I was in first grade my best friends Gary and Greg, who were twins, would come home from Christian Sunday School smiling and talking about God. I wanted to go with them and told my parents, who ended up sending me to Hebrew School, which they hadn't planned on doing, Mom told me later. One day Nanny, my mother's mother, was visiting, and I asked her if she believed in God. "Only stupid people do!" Being vision-impaired, a sissy, and bad at sports, the only thing I had going for me was being one of the smartest kids in my class – so, good-bye God! Then a few years later, after a relative died, I asked Nanny what happens to us when we die, thinking of my own unspoken memories of other lives. Her answer: "They bury you in the ground and you rot away!" made me try to bury my memories even more deeply.

I wonder what my life would have been like if the traditional Jewish teachings on prophecy, our rabbis hearing God's voice, and our writings on *gilgul*, reincarnation, had been a part of my parents' and Hebrew School teachers' lives, but they weren't, and over the years I've often found myself singing the chorus of Paul Simon's 1975 song of the same title: "Still crazy after all these years." Crazy. And accomplished. In addition to being a co-author of the international bestseller *Ask Your Angels,* a guide to opening up to and working with your own guardian angel, and the author of *Angel Answers,* which contains messages from my angel, and *Revelations for a New Millennium,* which includes messages from a range of guides, angels, and from God, I've written and co-written sixteen other published books. Five of them are queerish and Jewish, two are kids' picture books, and three are for gay men, with stories, poems, prayers, and essays in various anthologies and websites. But recently, in a conversation with my therapist, I prefaced something my guardian angel said to me that week with these words: "While I was meditating. Or, having a psychotic delusion," which made her laugh, as I hoped I would.

I also wonder what my life would have been like if someone had shared with me Mahatma Gandhi's thoughts on his own inner voices. He wrote: "There is no question of hallucination. I have stated a simple scientific truth, thus to be tested by all who have the will and the patience to acquire the necessary qualifications." A scientific truth.

Three times in my teens I dreamed that I was a teenage girl taking care of Gandhi when he was an old man, and as I've gotten older, from time to time when I don't have a beard, people have come up to me and said: "Has anyone told you how much you look like Gandhi?" There's a wonderful life-size statue of him behind the Ferry Building in San Francisco, done by Zlatko Punov and Steve Lowe. A few months ago I was looking up at him when a family from India came up to ask if they could take our picture, "Because you look just like him!"

○

I started writing stories in college, which I slowly gathered into a book called *little pictures.* I worked on those stories for fourteen years, inspired by a book my mother read to me when I was small, *Little Pictures of Japan,* that her mother read to her when she was small. It's a collection of translated haikus about the world of nature, selected by Olive Beaupré Miller and illustrated by Katharine Sturges. As you can see from the title of my book, *little pictures,* there are no capital letters in it. Their absence wasn't inspired by author and painter e e cummings, who didn't use them, but by the fact that I have a learning disability called dysgraphia. When I told my father in college that I wanted to be a writer he told me I'd have to learn to type, and when I moved to my first apartment he gave me his old manual typewriter and a book of typing lessons. Because of my dysgraphia it took me ten years to become a good typist, to this day I struggle to type capital letters, and all my first drafts and emails are written without them. (I don't text at all. Too hard to see and do!)

When *little pictures* and the drawings I did for it felt complete, back in the mid 1980s, I gave it to my wonderful editor friend Cheryl Woodruff, who's still a good friend. She passed the manuscript on to Chris Cox, her colleague at Ballantine Books – who loved it! Chris was a member of the noted gay writers group The Violet Quill, and *little pictures* came out in 1987 from the imprint he started, Available Books. Then I began to work on a sequel, called *Twenty-Two Views of a Life*, a memoir told through the rooms in my apartment, the objects in them, and the parts of my body, which Chris was planning to publish. Sadly, he died of AIDS in 1990, the imprint he started at Ballantine died with him, and I put the manuscript away, never to be published. Yet. But I've never stopped writing. Stories, essays, prayers, poems, novels. I'm in notebook 171 of my journal, which I began in college, and I continue to take dictation from my guides, angels, and from God.

Over the years I've made lists and written brief descriptions of the transformative experiences of my life, one called "Moments of Seeing," inspired by Virginia Woolf's expression "moments of being," from a collection of her writings with that title that was published after her death. (In *Ever After* I tell a story in which she lived much longer, wrote more, and lived happily ever after, with another woman.) At various times I thought about expanding the stories in my lists, but never did. Then Covid came to live with us, the nightmare wars in Ukraine and the Middle East followed, and with climate change threatening us all, I was meditating one morning when Goddess said to me: "It's time to collect those mystical experiences into a book about your amazing journey to Now."

Now. Wow. That was not what I was thinking about doing, but hearing Her words and telling these stories is about starting the final chapter in my life – by being more fully in the present in my body than I've ever been before. By writing about past lives – to be in this one. And by dancing with angels – so that I can dance with you!

Now.

I've gone on week-long retreats, but never lived in a beautiful ashram out in the woods somewhere, like many people I know have done. Near the end of his life my post-Orthodox dad had a guru, Rajneesh, today more commonly known as Osho, while my brother was a follower of Swami Muktananda. But I've never had a guru or done the things you might think would have led to my mystical experiences. No. I'm just a big old city boy, wandering through the world with a set of ancient gifts, here on an amazing journey, the major adventures of which I'll be sharing with you in your own unfolding journey, through a series of spiraling not-always-linear stories about the magical, mystical things that have happened to this old man. Who's sitting at his desk, looking out over his laptop – which he bought in 2011 but likes to say he bought in 1928 – looking over puddles on the flat roof of the apartment building next door, out to the Cathedral of Christ the Light, a few tall building in downtown Oakland, some beautiful trees, a sliver of Lake Merritt, and Fairyland – just out of sight.

PART 1

Living at Home

CHAPTER 1

The Story of My Arrival

JAPANESE AUTHOR YUKIO MISHIMA remembered his birth, which he wove into his second novel, *Confessions of a Mask,* the story of a closeted young gay man. I don't remember my birth, but I do remember floating in the womb, sealed, safe, contained, and cared for. I remember the sounds around me, throbbing, gurgling, the more distant sounds of talking, music, and I also remember that floating beside me, just to my left, was my travel companion – my twin. Yes, I remember him. Remember the two of us, two tiny not yet fully human-shaped beings, floating side by side, hearts beating, bodies pulsing, our cells being nourished by Mommy as we slowly grew. And I remember a moment, the two of us floating in that warm inward sea, when there was a surge, a throb, a jolt, a contraction. And all of a sudden – there was no life beside me, just an empty shape – and I was alone!

To this very day I can feel an absence beside me, just to my left. When I'm sitting, standing, out walking in the world, and over the years I've talked with four other people who have had the exact same experience. There have been times over the years when I've been angry at my twin brother – for leaving me alone with our crazy parents – and angry at him for not taking me with him! And I've wondered if my dance of accepting who I am and rejecting who I am is related to him. A deep inborn two-fold sense of me and not-me. And I've wondered if his absence has been the motivation behind my trying to live my life double. As artist and writer. Writer and teacher. Teacher and body-worker. Walker and sitter. Dancer and singer. Realist and dreamer. Celebrant and mourner. Old man and womb-floater. Doubter, believer. Accepter, denier. Both in and out of the world.

Although I always felt him, his presence and absence, I was around three years old when someone told me the story about him, perhaps my mother, or more likely my unboundaried Nanny – but no one ever talked about him again, and I knew that I wasn't supposed to either. When I was four or five, wanting him to be more present, I started calling him Alexander, the name of Nanny's father, who I was named after. So it was the two of us, Andy and Alexander.

As a teen I came up with two theories as to why no one ever talked about him. First – no one I've ever met who wasn't a twin themself ever set out to have twins. People just want to have "a baby," and after four years of marriage my parents were ready to do that, have that. And second – my mother's older sister had a miscarriage between my cousins Michael and Eileen – and from the way that Aunt Myra talked about Gregory I always imagined that he was two or three when he died. But when I was six or seven I asked Mommy about him and she told me what really happened. Thus my second theory – Mom didn't want to make a cult out of her lost baby the way that her sister had.

In 1965 a book of photographs by Leonard Nilsson was published called *A Child Is Born* that charts human development from conception to birth. Flipping through it I came upon a picture of a fetus at the beginning of its second trimester – and it looked exactly like what I felt and remembered about Alexander and me when he died.

I always missed him and when I was in my mid-twenties I asked my gay therapist if my attraction to other boys and men might come from wanting to find a replacement for him. My therapist's reply was: "Most of my patients are gay men, and I've never heard anyone else ever tell me a story like yours. So my answer to your question is – no. You're gay because you're gay, not because you're a surviving twin."

Some time later I brought Alexander up again and my therapist suggested that it might be time to talk about him with my mother. At that point I was living in Brooklyn and Mom was living in California. One morning when I was visiting, we were sitting in her combination kitchen and family room and I nervously brought up the subject. To my great relief Mom said that she was open to talking about him. I was sitting in a straight-back wooden kitchen chair and she was sitting a few feet away in a big padded Danish Modern recliner, with sunlight pouring in through the sliding doors to the back patio.

"After four years of marriage your father and I were ready to start a family. So I stopped using my diaphragm. But I'd always had very irregular periods. One and then another two months later, then another three weeks later, and then one three months after that. So I wasn't showing, and I couldn't tell if I'd missed one."

"One day your father and I were out playing tennis and I began to hemorrhage. He rushed me to the hospital where they told me either, 'Good news lady, you're pregnant. And bad news lady, you're miscarrying.' Or 'Bad news lady, you're miscarrying. But good news lady, you're still pregnant!' I can't remember which."

Mom was quiet for a while and then I nervously asked why no one ever talked about what happened, or talked about my twin. She gave me a sad sweet smile and said, tenderly, "I guess I never really thought about him, or talked about him – because I didn't know he existed until he was gone – and because I had *you*!"

Pausing, excited and nervous, sad and moved, I thanked her for talking about him, told her that I'd been calling him Alexander since I was a little boy, and asked what she would have called him if he had lived. Mom leaned all the way back in her reclining chair and sat silently for about three minutes, which was the longest I'd ever seen her being still till I was looking down at her in her coffin many years later. Her eyes were closed and she was stretched out with her bare feet pointing toward me, while I sat across from her, leaning forward, eager, waiting.

All at once she sat up, grinning, looked me right in the eyes and said – "Benjamin."

Some years before, I'd gone on a trip to Sedona, Arizona and brought back two small red stones that were still sitting on a shelf in my old bedroom in her house. One of them looked like a mountain, flat on the bottom and pointy on top, and the other looked like a gravestone, flat on the bottom and curved on top. I took that little rounded stone, about an inch and a half tall, and wrote on it with a black marking pen:

Benjamin Ramer
1950

That afternoon I walked down the block to water, in Seal Beach, California, where Mom was living at the time, did a made-up-on-the-spot memorial service, and tossed that sweet little red rock into the Pacific Ocean, feeling a sad sweet dance of joy and sorrow in my grateful grieving body. And from that time on I've called him Benjamin.

○

When I was born, the nurses in the hospital wrapped me in a yellow blanket. My parents told this story over and over again, and I tell it at length in *Two Hearts Dancing*.

That story haunted me all through my childhood. In the schoolyard, where I sat alone under a tree, watching the boys play baseball in one corner, while the girls jumped rope in another. It haunted me in the bathtub. It haunted me in my dreams. And it haunted me later, when the hair started growing on my upper lip, in my armpits, beneath my Fruit of the Loom white jockey underpants. Because I looked around me, I looked everywhere, and I didn't see anyone else quite like me. Wrapped up in yellow. Chicken. Scared.

When I was born, six pounds and seven brown ounces, with a head of curly thick black hair, the nurses in the hospital wrapped me in a yellow blanket. And I'm wrapped in it still. And to this very day I wonder – how did those nurses know, when they wrapped me, newly slipped into this world and still jet-lagged, how did they know, on that new spring night in 1951 – when there were no other choices but pink and blue – that I would be as different as I am?

CHAPTER 2

How I Learned to Individuate

I WAS ALMOST THREE when my little brother was born. I felt like such a big boy, because Daddy and Mommy got me my first bed so that Richie could sleep in the crib on the opposite wall where I used to sleep. I remember waking up in that little bed, rolling over, stretching and opening my eyes to another day – not quite certain of who I was – waking up from what I can only describe as "a pool of selves."

There were six or seven or eight of them, of us – and I knew that they were all me, different me's, living in places unlike any that I had ever seen, back in the days when very few people had televisions, when my family was so poor that we almost never went on vacation, or even to the movies.

One me lived on a small tropical island. One me lived in a dense jungle. One me lived near a tall green mountain. And one me lived in a great big house unlike any house that I had ever yet seen, with many rooms, many floors, and with different parents, grandparents, two older sisters, and lots of servants – servants something little Andy didn't yet know existed. So I'd wake up in that pool of me's, and feel them and be them. I could hear them/me/us speak different languages, none that I'd ever yet heard, and sometimes I would dream about them, and sometimes I would dream *as* them! I would dream that I was walking in a jungle, sitting by a stream, sitting with a different set of parents in that great big house somewhere, or another house that we went to for the summer in a horse-drawn carriage in another life. And on other worlds. I still remember once being in my stroller, out at night, which was rare for me, looking up and all around the dark sky, then turning back behind me and asking, "Mommy, what happened to the other moons?"

Each morning it took me a little while to orient myself. I would stretch and yawn and look around the room, at my baby brother, still asleep in the crib on the opposite wall, that crib which used to be mine. I'd roll over, stretch, and say to myself as my Self became more clear, "I am the little boy who lives in *this* apartment with *that* new baby brother and with *that* Mommy and Daddy who are still asleep in the other room."

Then there was a morning, a morning when I was around three and a half, and I woke up in that pool of selves. Villa. Grass hut. Ocean. Jungle. And when I stretched and rolled around – my pajama top slid off my left shoulder – and I saw something that I had never noticed before – a small brown mole on my left shoulder! I remember looking at it, rubbing it, smiling as I pulled my pajama top back up over my shoulder, covering it. I didn't talk about it with anyone, but for the next few days, each time I woke up I would pull down my pajama top, look at and rub the mole on my left shoulder, and say to myself – "Yes, I am the little boy who lives in this apartment with my baby brother and our parents. Yes. I am *this* me. The one right here. I am this me. I am Andy."

Each day I'd wake up and go through that little ritual, little routine, getting more and more grounded in my little Andy body, getting more and more accustomed to being my little Andy self. Which got me to a time when I was so much more me, so much more *this* me – that I didn't need to look at my shoulder anymore. And from that morning on I'd wake up as myself, as one self, never forgetting the other selves that I had been, but for the first time clearly focused in my body, in my bed, with my family, in our apartment, in the world, as just one me, little Andy.

○

Around that time I remember standing in the living room of our Elmhurst, Queens apartment, looking up at my mother, thinking of the people I lived with in that huge old house, and I asked her, "Mommy, what happened to my other parents?" She said nothing, but the rage coming out of her body toward me was such that I never once ever talked about my memories, my dreams, my experiences again with anyone. When I was older I came up with two theories about my mother's rage. One, that she felt totally inadequate as a parent and heard my question as an inquiry about my "better" parents, as a kind of rejection. And two, that she looked down at me and thought – "Oh my God, (not that she believed in God, but) my kid is crazy!"

Once when Nanny and I were alone – ironically, my atheist anti-religious Nanny – she gave me my first and only clue for years. She reminded me that I was named after her father, told me that when someone died their soul went into the body of the person who was named for them, and when no one else was around Nanny would tenderly call me "Little Father." It was only in my freshman year in college that I heard about and began to read about reincarnation. And it was only in 1997 when I read Carol Bowman's book *Children's Past Lives,* where she talks about interviewing people from cultures where they *do* believe in reincarnation, that I could imagine a different story:

"Mommy, what happened to my other parents?"

"Oh Sweetheart," Mommy says, kneeling down in front of me and lovingly placing her hands on my tiny shoulders. "Tell me about them. What were they like? Do you remember where you lived? Maybe I knew them, and maybe I knew you too!"

Over the years I've met and read about other people who've had the kinds of experiences and memories that I'm sharing with you, and I've come to believe that every single one of us have them. But because we live in a society that doesn't honor or respect them – most of us forget them.

○

Dr. Jim Tucker, who's been interviewing kids who remember their past lives since 1998, and wrote about his findings in *Life Before Life,* discovered that for most of them/us, such memories begin to fade around age three. But mine didn't.

CHAPTER 3

A Tale of Luminosity

NOT LONG AFTER I'D SOLIDIFIED into being just one me, still with my memories and dreams, I had an experience that I've always remembered.

It's the middle of the night. Baby Richie is sound asleep. I'm in my pajamas and standing up on my bed, looking at the closed door to the hallway that led to the living room where Mommy and Daddy slept in their bed behind a bookcase.

It's the middle of the night. The tiny night-light in the wall across from my bed is on, to the left of the closed door to the hallway.

It's the middle of the night. I'm wide awake and standing on my bed. And the room, the little bedroom that I shared with my baby brother – is filled with a luminous white-gold light that I'm looking out into, amazed and delighted.

○

That's the entire memory, which is only six or seven seconds long. Just me standing there on the top of my blanket, looking out at the light across from me. I don't know what happened before it, and I have no memory of how or when I went back to sleep. That's all that I remember. Me. And the light. It was only when I was in my mid-twenties, living in Brooklyn, and an angel appeared to me while I was sitting on the parquet floor meditating, a story that you'll read about a bit later, followed by visits from other angels, that I realized that what had happened to me when I was just a little boy – was a visit from my own guardian/companion angel, Sargolais, who you'll also be hearing more about in this book.

CHAPTER 4

There and Back Again

I ADORED NANNY'S MOTHER, who we all called Baba, Yiddish for grandmother. She died when I was three. I was named Andrew after her husband, Nanny's father, Alexander Gilman, who died not long before my mother was pregnant with me. Everyone called him Zayda, which means grandfather in Yiddish. His Hebrew name was Shabtai, as was Baba's mother's father, a rabbi from the Caucasus, and Nanny told me that I was named for both of them in Hebrew. So I call myself Shabtai Three, call my great grandfather Shabtai Two, call my great great great grandfather Shabtai One, and keep old black-and-white photographs of the two of them on a shelf in my bedroom closet that I call my ancestor shrine, along with photos of all the other ancestors I have pictures of.

From the time that I was very small I would sometimes feel Shabtai One around me and sometimes he would come with Beata, Nanny's older sister, who died before Nanny was born. I knew her from another picture, the originals of which I've had since Nanny died and Mom passed them on to me, pictures mounted on cardboard, both of them taken in Odessa in the late 1800s. Shabtai and Beata were sweet and comforting and seemed to always know when I needed support. And from the start I knew enough to never talk about them, not even with Nanny. Or to tell anyone about the other me's or about the other people who would sometimes talk to me, awake and in my dreams. Because I'd already learned that parents who find it sweet when their little children have imaginary playmates, if they keep talking to people who aren't there when they get older – freak out and think they're crazy. And I was already different enough. A sissy. Not a little girl like most of my cousins, but not quite a boy either. So the last thing I wanted was to be thought crazy.

When I was around three years old I got pneumonia. I remember lying on top of a blanket on Mommy and Daddy's big bed in the living room, with Mommy sitting right beside me, her hand on my chest. One moment I was looking up at her, drenched in sweat, and the next moment I was out of my body, floating in space. And then Zayda came toward me. I recognized him from the pictures of him that everyone had in my family. He looked down at me, smiling, said, "It's not your time to be here yet," and escorted me back to my body. I returned with a jolt to find Mommy leaning over me, her hand on my neck, with a look of terror on her face that I'd never seen before or since on the face of anyone else except in a movie. Terror, and then relief, as she felt my pulse come back. Then she leaned toward me, trembling, sobbing, and wrapped her loving arms around me and pulled me to her chest.

○

That was my first big journey. It was only when I was in my late twenties that I ever heard anyone talk about NDE's, Near Death Experiences. What a comfort. To hear about, read about, other peoples' stories just like mine and know that I was not alone.

CHAPTER 5

Four Tales of Fracturing

ONCE THE WORLD WAS WHOLE and one and I was one with it. I still remember how that felt. Holy.

○

In the 1950s all shampoo stung your eyes. At night, whenever Mommy gave me a bath, she would tell me to close my eyes before she lathered up my head. One night I didn't close them fast enough and shampoo got in my eyes. I yelled "Ow!" Started flailing. And when Mommy lowered me into the tub water to rinse off my head she was shaking with rage and pushed me into the water and held me down on the bottom of the tub! I started to struggle, choking, unable to breathe, gagging on water, when she panicked at what she was doing, yanked me up, gasping and coughing out water. She yelled for my father, who came running in and took over, which he'd never done before, or ever again, and she dashed out of the bathroom and didn't come back. This is something that we never talked about, then or ever. That fracture between boy and his Mommy.

○

Back in those days there were laundry rooms with washing machines in them in all the apartment buildings my relatives lived in, but there were no dryers yet. The laundry rooms had clotheslines for hanging up wet clothes in winter and when it was raining, and lines up on the roof that we would use when it was sunny and warm out.

One day I went with Mommy up to the roof, she carrying a big straw basket with our clothes in it, and I handed her each wet garment to hang on the lines. That evening when Daddy came home from work we went up to the roof to get them, and as we were leaving he said, "Oh look! There's Mars!" He pointed up at the darkening sky and said, "That red star." Well, I saw nothing red like one of my Crayola crayons, said so, and Daddy put down the straw clothing basket, knelt beside me, and pointed. I still didn't see anything red, said so again, so Daddy took my right hand and pointed it up to the sky, but in the flickering of stars I still didn't see anything red, and said so again. I could feel Daddy's fury rising up in his body as he jerked my hand again, pointing, and said, "It's right over there!"

In that moment the whole world shattered for me, the holy wholeness that was all I had ever known and experienced. Because I realized that if I said, "Oh. Now I see it, Daddy!" – he would stop being angry. So I said it. He let go of my hand, smiled at me, got up, picked up the laundry basket and led me back to the elevator to go downstairs.

○

We were too poor to go on vacations, but Uncle Bob and Aunt Rachie had a little cabin at a place called Lake Cherokee, and we went to visit them that summer. One day Daddy and I were out on the lake in a canoe, me behind him as he rowed. I loved being out on the water, gliding, looking out at the trees, the people on the shore, the clear gorgeous sky. All of a sudden he said, "Look! A deer!" I loved the story of Bambi, but had never seen a live deer and said, "Where?" He pointed again, but I didn't see it and said so, and he pointed again. Again I said I didn't see it and I could feel the canoe start shaking as he pointed again and nearly shouted, "It's right over there, next to the waterfall!" Well, I couldn't see the waterfall *or* the deer, but suddenly the world split in two again and, terrified of Daddy and the shaking canoe I said, "Oh yes. Now I see it!" And Daddy calmed down, the canoe stopped shaking, he went back to rowing us across the water, and all was well – and not well at all. My whole world fractured. Two, not one.

I don't remember what my third lie was. Lying became a part of my reality. Something I knew how to do when I had to, to protect myself.

○

Nanny and Grandpa Lester split up when Mommy was five, and we rarely ever saw him or Anna his second wife.

I was always a bit scared of Daddy's mom Rose, who we called Grandma, but I adored Daddy's father Max, who we just called Grandpa. Grandpa was a simple man, a little shorter than Grandma. Each morning after he did his morning prayers he read the Yiddish paper, but unlike at Nanny's Bensonhurst, Brooklyn apartment around the corner, which was filled with art on the walls and shelves of books in several languages, the only art in Grandma and Grandpa's apartment was a framed picture that Daddy gave them when he was in high school, and the only book they had was Grandpa's prayer book.

One day shortly before Richie was born, Grandma and I were sitting at her tiny kitchen table. I was sitting on a phone book, eating a bowl of soup. In the middle of the table was an old mayonnaise jar filled with water, with a bunch of flowers in it. I don't remember what kind, but they were flat-petaled, perhaps some kind of poppy.

I was sitting at the table. With a bowl of soup in front of me. And the flowers, mostly red and yellow, were making such a wonderful sound that I looked up from my bowl of soup and said, "Grandma, the flowers sound pretty."

Grandma had a Yiddish accent thick enough to cut a cabbage with, and her English wasn't very good. But she leaned in my direction, smiling, and in a loud voice said, "Flowers look pretty and smell pretty. Pictures look pretty. Music sounds pretty."

It was a lecture on the appropriate use of my senses, and I turned to her and said, "I know that Grandma. But the flowers *sound* pretty too."

Grandma was a bit annoyed. She didn't take well to back-talk. But she looked at me indulgently. Smiled again at her dense little grandson who was obviously in need of a little more clarification, and repeated, in a louder voice, as if I were senile or hard of hearing: "Flowers look pretty and smell pretty. Pictures look pretty. Music sounds pretty."

I could feel her irritation as clearly as I could hear the flowers humming with a sound as clear to me as their fragrance. And once again, I repeated myself. And once again, her large fleshy face glaring down at me, furious that her supposedly smart little grandson, the one whose "Regulah Yenkee noze" she liked to show off to her girlfriends, was having such a difficult time learning how to speak – no, to think – Grandma repeated herself. Loudly and very slowly, one word at a time. "Flowers – look – pretty – and – smell – pretty! Pictures – look – pretty! Music – sounds – pretty!"

I was scared of her anger and looked away from her, at the wall behind her, then over the table and out the window across from me. And something shifted in me, some deep and willful brain-sense shifted – and I shut down my capacity to hear the flowers.

○

All these many years later, I've never heard another flower singing – but when I hold my hands over them, or over any growing thing – plants, animals, people – I feel them vibrating. Lest you think my memories of Grandma are only negative, she left me with two gifts. One: She once told me, "After Shabbos, Tuesday is the second holiest day of the week. It was only on Tuesday that God said twice "ki tov! – it's good!" about what He had made," referring to the creation story in the Torah. Shabbos, Shabbat, the Sabbath. Then she added that in the village she came from everyone got married on Tuesday. And Two: Grandma and I were walking to my cousin Larry's bar mitzvah when it started to rain. I got very upset and she said, "When it rains on a special day it means that God is blessing it!" And I realize now that these fracturings have helped to shape me the way that Michelangelo's chisel helped him to create his gorgeous statue of David.

CHAPTER 6

My First Realization

IT WAS HALLOWEEN. Richie was very little and I was in nursery school. The school was run by two women who were sisters, from France. They spoke English in a way that was for me half-way to music, and their school was in a big old house with fancy walls and doors and moldings, and all of our cubby-holes were painted different colors.

It was Halloween and we were going to have a party. I had probably worn a Halloween costume the year before, but I didn't remember it and wasn't old enough to understand what the holiday was about or why I had to wear a costume. But all the other kids were going to wear one. It was fun, exciting. Who would have the best costume?

Daddy came home from work one evening with a mask. It was a face, a strange face with a big nose. It was scary, and I liked it. But Daddy didn't. So that night, when baby Richie was asleep, Daddy sat at his desk, took his paints out, and decided to change that fierce face.

Today we have spray paints and air brushes. In those days the tools were basic, simple. I stood on my tippy toes at Daddy's right, watching him dip a six inch metal tube skinnier than a drinking straw, with a little stick-out handle on it, into jars of paint of different colors. He would suck the paint up into the stick, then blow it out on the mask, and then do it all over again with a different color in a different place.

Dip it over and over again. Blow through it over and over, spraying out colors. Till layers of paint covered up the face that the mask had come with. Slowly and carefully Daddy repainted the molded plastic face to suit him. Painted a new face on that mask. As I stood in the pool of light cast by his desk lamp. Stood in silence. Watching him.

Watching him? I was captivated, consumed, awakened. I loved to draw and paint. I had boxes of crayons, paints, a little easel and a big pad to fill with colors. And yet – I had never seen anyone make anything. I had never seen magic, never seen anyone make art. Only play, with colors.

Drawing and painting for me were like talking or walking or eating. Spontaneous. Instinctual. I did them. It happened. I scrawled. I scratched. But for the first time, watching my father paint, I understood what it meant to make something. To do something with intention. To see something. To shape something. To impose your will on it. For the very first time – I knew about creation. And that night the magic of his hands opened my left eye. The one nearest to him.

I have never forgotten that night. The artist in me was conceived in that pool of incandescent light. Watching him paint that mask, and then make a pointed hat for me to wear, out of black construction paper.

None of us had store-bought costumes. All the other kids' mommies made theirs. But it was my daddy who made mine. He took one of his old black turtleneck shirts, wrapped it around me and tied it around my waist with one of his narrow black ties. Then he put the mask on me, the mask he painted bluish, a witch's face, then he put the pointed hat on my little head of curly dark hair. Did I have the best costume? That, I can't remember. Only this story. Of the creative, perhaps perceptive Daddy, who sent his little odd boy off to nursery school as he did. Looking a bit like the Wicked Witch of the West in *The Wizard of Oz* – pronoun she – only smiling, and blue-faced, and not wicked at all.

○

Part of my morning mediation practice is to sit with pad and colored pencils and do a little drawing. Thank you Daddy for guiding me on this path.

CHAPTER 7

Learning to be Present

EVERYTHING ABOUT GRANDPA WAS SLOW, slower than anyone I've ever met. When he talked, with a heavy Yiddish accent, there was a period after every word. When he sneezed he began with a series of tiny slow hissing sounds followed by one soft slightly louder one. And when Grandpa walked, he walked more slowly than anyone else. We would leave their apartment together, holding hands as we went down the stairs. But when we got outside it only took a few steps for me to break away, run down the path in front of their little apartment building to the sidewalk, and then run back and take his hand again. Then we'd walk a few more steps, but I'd get restless and dash off. Being a good boy, when Grandpa finally got to the sidewalk I'd run to the corner, but I never ran into the street. I always turned back. And I'd continue racing back and forth until Grandpa finally made it to the corner himself, where I'd take his hand again as we turned the corner heading toward 86th Street, and then I'd do the same dance. Racing back and forth as he continued his slow journey forward.

When I got older I liked to walk with Grandpa even more. Grandma was always telling me what to do, what to play, what to eat. Grandpa said nothing and asked nothing. But then again, walking with him was torture. Because I knew that he wanted to hold my hand. And I was too young, too fast, too impatient. I'd try to stay with him. But it hurt to move that slowly. And Grandpa wasn't even that old then. He was in his early sixties.

One day when I was around five Grandpa and I went out for one of our walks. It was early spring, not too hot yet. I had on a sweater. So did Grandpa, only he called his a cardigan, just as he called the record player a victrola and his suitcase a valise. We walked down the path in front of their building, and I remember to this day how we turned left on the sidewalk and slowly headed toward the corner, our usual route. I remember holding his hand till I couldn't stand it anymore, and then I broke away, ran to the corner, then back to him, and took his hand again, only to walk a few more paces and dart away.

On the third time, when I came back to him and put my little right hand in his bigger left one, Grandpa clutched onto me and wouldn't let go. I struggled a little, trying to pull away, wanting to run back to the corner, wiggling my hand in his. And then something happened. Something shifted. And I was walking hand-in-hand with Grandpa – but I no longer wanted to run ahead. No. I was walking just as slowly as he was. And it was easy. I flowed. I flowed with him.

As we walked down 82nd Street toward 21st Avenue I looked to my right and noticed the tree in front of his building, a little to the left of the front path, in the dirt between the sidewalk and the curb. One day not too long before I'd come home from nursery school with a picture of a tree that I was very proud of. Daddy laughed at the green circle with a brown line beneath it and said, "What that? A lollipop?" Well, it looked like a tree to me! And when he took out some paper and drew me a "real" tree, with roots and trunk and branches and leaves, I could see it but couldn't relate to it.

But that day, as I walked hand-in-hand with Grandpa, I saw the tree! I saw it as it really was. I saw its roots coming up from under the sidewalk. I saw its bark, dark and crackly. I saw the wildly irregular upward thrust of its branches. I saw the flutter of green leaves above us, and the way that its leaves and branches wove themselves together as we slow slow slowly walked hand in hand to the corner, where we turned left and headed toward 86th Street, our usual destination.

For the very first time, as we walked, everything was alive. Real. And everything was intensely beautiful. I looked up at Grandpa and smiled. He pressed my hand and pulled me a little closer to him, so that my little left hand in his much bigger right one rubbed against the side of his black pants, which he called trousers. Did he know that I was seeing? I'm not sure, but I think so. I think he felt the change in me. And was he seeing the same way, seeing the world the same way? I think so, being a silent see-er himself. The two of us walking together. Seeing together. Under the trees, real trees.

○

My freshman college roommate Erick opened the door to spirituality for me, a word that I'd never heard before, back in 1969. Tragically, he died three weeks after freshman year ended, and the following year, bereft, I stepped further into the journey he started me on by taking a Sociology of Religion class. Rather than meet in a classroom we met out in an empty field near campus, sitting barefoot on the grass. And rather than being an academic venture, our professor, Houston Wood crafted a class that was experiential. There were no tests. Our only assignment was to keep a journal. I had always wanted to keep one, have been keeping it ever since, as I mentioned before.

Early in the semester Houston taught us a series of Hindu mantras that we would chant at the beginning and the end of each class, and one day he taught us how to meditate. As he slowly guided us through the process, and as I deepened into it, I realized to my great amazement and delight – that I already knew how to meditate! – from walking with Grandpa, and from decades of doing it myself – walking alone among my tree siblings, praying with my legs, whenever I was feeling anxious, afraid, angry, confused, and in need of grounding and comfort.

CHAPTER 8

Hello and Good-bye

GRANDPA LOVED BIRDS. Grandma didn't, but when he brought home a parakeet in a cage one day, being a dutiful wife of the 1950s, Grandma insisted on taking care of him. When it was time to clean his cage she'd let him out so that he could fly around the living room. One day he refused to go back in his cage and when Grandma grabbed him in the air – she pulled out all of his tail feathers, which never grew back, and that little bird was soon given to me, my very first pet.

I don't remember what if anything Grandpa called him, but I called him Chirpy after a bird that Nanny had. Chirpy lived in a cage on the dresser along the wall at the foot of my bed, and unlike his being able to fly around Grandma and Grandpa's living room, in our apartment Chirpy was never allowed out of his cage. Mommy cleaned his cage and showed me how to feed him, and I loved sitting on the edge of the bed talking to him and listening to him talk back.

Just before I was tucked in each night, just before Mommy or Daddy read me or told me a story, one of them would put a white kitchen towel over Chirpy's cage and he would go to sleep.

One morning I woke up – and Chirpy's cage was gone! I ran into the kitchen where I could hear Mommy and Daddy talking, over breakfast and coffee.

"Where's Chirpy?"

Daddy took me up in his lap and wrapped an arm around me.

"Chirpy died while you were sleeping."

"Died?"

"Yes, he died in the night, Sweetheart."

"But where is he?"

"I just told you. He died."

"I know that. But where is he?"

Daddy pushed me back from him a little bit and said, after a short pause, "I buried him in the yard, under the bushes."

There was a small narrow yard behind our apartment building that we kids liked to play in, and at one end of it there was a line of tall bushes. I quickly got dressed and took the elevator down, finally old enough to reach the buttons myself, ran out to the yard and looked all through the bushes, poking in the dirt, but I couldn't find Chirpy anywhere.

Back upstairs in our apartment I told Daddy that I couldn't find him, and asked "When will he be back?"

Daddy looked at me with a sad sweet look and said, "I told you Sweetheart. Chirpy died."

I looked up at him and asked again, "I know that. But when will he be back?"

With a familiar sound of annoyance in his voice, Daddy looked down at me and said again, "I already told you. He won't be back."

And I looked up at him in puzzlement. Remembering having died myself, several times, and then come back, I couldn't understand how a grown-up who was supposed to be so much smarter than a little kid like me didn't know that.

○

When I was in college I talked about that morning with my father, he told me that he lied to me about where he'd buried Chirpy, because he didn't want me to find his body. Feeling brave, I told him my own true story. Which he was then able to hear, given the changes in his own life over time.

○

When we moved to the suburbs, which I'll be telling you more about soon, I carried this experience with me. In those days I didn't know any kids who had dogs or cats, but we all had goldfish, one at a time in little round glass bowls, and little turtles who lived in plastic bowls with water on the bottom and a small island in the middle that had a plastic palm tree sticking up from it, and some of us had birds too, parakeets and canaries. When our goldfish died our parents flushed them down the toilet. They disposed of our other little pets by wrapping them in newspaper and sticking them in the garbage.

I was in first grade when my goldfish died, and I decided to bury it in the yard, back behind the garage. I dug a hole and wrote its name on a rock that I placed on top of its grave, and then I did a little made-up-on-the-spot ceremony for it. I'd never been to a funeral, but some part of me remembered how to officiate at one, when I was six years old. We had a little rabbit for a while and when it died I buried it in another place in the yard, and being larger than a fish or a turtle or a little bird I made a wooden cross to put on its grave. I'd never been to a funeral but we'd driven by cemeteries filled with crosses. When my mother and visiting Aunt Myra saw it they teased me, reminding me that we were Jewish without helping me understand why making a cross was wrong. I tried to defend myself, which didn't work, and never made a cross again.

When other kids in the neighborhood had pets that died I offered to do the same thing. I'd make little coffins for them out of cardboard, bury them, write their names on a rock, and do a little good-bye ceremony for them. My parents were okay about my doing that, but forbade me to do it for rabbits or dogs or cats. Only for little pets. The snows of winter moved all the stones around so I made a map of the cemetery, with each pet's name on it, so that I could put the stones back in their right places when it was spring again.

I never talked with my parents about my doing this, and to this day I wonder what it was like for them to stand at the edge of the yard watching their six, seven, eight, nine year old little boy officiating at pet funerals.

CHAPTER 9

The First Time I Stepped into Memory

DADDY LOVED TO DRAW and paint and worked as an interior designer, although I sometimes lie and tell people he was an architect like my brother. When I was old enough to go into Manhattan with Daddy he would take me to art galleries and museums. One weekend we got on the subway – always a big treat for me – I loved standing on the seat and looking out into the dark tunnel – and we went to see a show that he was very excited about, at the Museum of Modern Art.

I remember holding his hand as we walked from the subway to the museum, and walked through the museum into the courtyard – not at a meditative pace! And there, right before us – was a house. A house unlike any house that I had ever seen in Queens or Brooklyn or Manhattan or on Staten Island, the only places that I knew. A house that Daddy told me was made in Japan and taken apart and sent all the way over here, where it was all put back together again. A house that somehow was familiar to me.

People were waiting to get into the house, but you couldn't go in until you took off your shoes and lined them up outside the door and put on a pair of brown paper slippers. I can see those slippers in my mind, the soft brown veined paper. I can see how they looked as we slipped them over our socks, and seventy years later I can still hear the soft crinkly sound they made as we slipped them on and walked with them on, from room to room of the big different beautiful house – a house that was utterly unlike anything that Andy had ever been in before – and yet a house that I innately understood. From my all-time favorite picture book, *Crow Boy*, written and illustrated by Taro Yashima. It's the story of an unpopular little boy that's set in Japan, a copy of which is sitting next to my laptop as I type, and from *Little Pictures of Japan,* which I talked about earlier.

The Japanese house was big, in a lovely garden, a much bigger house than any other house that I had ever seen or been to. And it was beautiful. Bright and open and different and beautiful. I wanted to live there. Because I loved that house. The sliding doors with paper in the panels, unlike any doors I'd ever seen before, as Andy. The woven mats on the floors. Never seen them either, as Andy. I was thrilled to be able to take home the paper slippers, which eventually fell apart, as I loved wearing them. But the house itself stayed with me. As those two beautiful picture books have. Because in a soft deep inward way as we walked around it, I remember that I'd once lived in a house rather like it, in one of the pool of lives that used to go dancing in me when I woke up each morning, till they didn't anymore.

○

Not long after Erick died I took a class in Asian Religions. One of our text-books was *The World of Zen: An East-West Anthology,* by Nancy Wilson Ross. Flipping through it I came upon a picture of that house! It had a name – Shofuso – Pine Breeze Villa. It was built in Nagoya, Japan as a traditional 17th century style nobleman's villa in 1953, as a gift in the post-war years from Japan to the people of the United States. I learned that after two years in the courtyard of the Museum of Modern Art it had been taken apart and rebuilt in Philadelphia. Had I known that – I would have gone to visit it again. Then again, I didn't have to. That beautiful house lives inside me!

CHAPTER 10

In Nanny's Garden

GRANDPA WAS QUIET. Grandma was chatty and controlling. Nanny was chatty and warm. She had long red fingernails and wavy dark hair. Whenever she found a gray one she'd make me pull it out. Grandpa and I had our walks, but there was always so much to do in Nanny's apartment that we'd rarely go outside. We'd string beads, bake cookies, play cards, look at family photographs, and Nanny liked to play music and tell me and read me stories. She didn't believe in children's books and read me from whatever she was reading herself, in the language it was written in: English, Russian, French. Dickens, Twain, Tolstoy, de Maupassant.

One day when I was four Nanny took me in her lap, looked down at me and said, "When I was your age men on horseback came into our village to kill all the Jews. Mama and Papa had a vegetable stall in the market. They were in the next town buying things and left me with our good Christian neighbors, who hid me at the bottom of their coal bin. If they hadn't, I wouldn't be here, your mother wouldn't be here, and you wouldn't be here."

She looked down at me, sternly, which wasn't like her, and then continued. "When they got back, Papa took me to the gymnasium. That's a word for a school. And he picked me up so that I could look over a big white folding screen. All the dead people were laid out in rows on the floor. Papa said that they were my people, and I should never forget. And that's why I'm telling you this now, so that you won't forget either."

Another day when I was staying with her, Nanny asked me if I wanted to go for a walk in the woods. We'd be gone for hours, so she packed her wooden picnic basket with sandwiches cut my favorite way, in half from corner to corner, and put in two tins of cookies she'd baked, one of sweet cookies and one of salty ones, to nibble on with our tea. She had two silver thermoses, one for her black tea and one for my colored tea. Sometimes it was bright red, or yellow, sometimes green, or orange. A little boy's tea that Nanny made with a teaspoon of Jell-O. I always got to pick the color.

The picnic basket was too heavy for me to carry, and even Nanny had to use both hands. The path was rocky and winding, and soon the hills rose up in front of us. Then we took a narrow path above a gorge with a river racing through it. That was the scary part. But we loved feeling the spray on our faces, and soon the path went downhill and we emerged at the edge of a broad meadow, a few horses nibbling grass in the distance. Beyond them was the forest, its trees so green and tall, and when we got closer we could hear the wind rustling the leaves, whispering, calling.

We followed a deer path that led to a small clearing and plunked down on the grass. It was my job to open the picnic basket and take everything out. I asked Nanny which plate and cup she wanted. To me they were pink and blue and green, but she called them rose and aqua and chartreuse. I liked my cup and plate to match, but she preferred two that didn't. Then I took out our sandwiches and we ate them, both of us tired and hungry from our long long walk.

When we were done with our sandwiches I took out the cookie tins as Nanny poured our tea and put cookies on our plates. First we had a sweet cookie and a sip of tea. Then we ate a salty one, with another sip of tea. So we were alternating till all the tea and cookies were gone, and then we stretched out on the grass so that we could feel the sun on our faces. We looked at the clouds and watched a family of cranes flying overhead. Then I crawled up in her lap and Nanny told me a story about her family, back in Russia, not a scary one, which made me happy.

Soon the sun began to sink in the sky and we knew it was time to head home. We put everything back in the picnic basket – and got up from the big Persian carpet on her living room floor that we'd been sitting on, resting on. An old red faded Persian carpet with a thick border of leaves that Nanny had turned into a wild forest, with a clearing in the center that I called Nanny's Garden. Not the first time we'd gone there.

Stretching, smiling, we got up and turned to the left to admire the reproduction of 19th century French artist Rosa Bonheur's painting *The Horse Fair*, hanging over a round marble table whose legs were three tall cranes carved from mahogany that had flown over us as we lay on the grass. We paused for a moment at the archway that divided the living and dining rooms, that Nanny turned into a deep gorge, walked by the tall bookcases she'd turned into tall mountains, then headed into the kitchen to unpack the picnic basket and do the dishes. Nanny washing. Me drying. In her five-room apartment in Bensonhurst, Brooklyn, in the city of New York.

CHAPTER 11

My Second Realization

SLOWLY OVER TIME DADDY'S design business grew, and he and Mommy bought a house in the suburbs, in Rockville Centre, Long Island. On moving day our little four-room apartment, the only home I ever knew, was filled with boxes. Mommy said that Richie and I could take one thing with us. He chose a stuffed animal. I kept out my world globe, my greatest treasure. Every night when Daddy came to tuck me in I would close my eyes, spin the globe, plunk down a finger, and wherever it landed, Daddy would tell me a story about that place. But in the rush and confusion, I forgot my globe and only remembered it as our car pulled out behind the moving van, me and Mommy crying, Richie sitting silent beside me, Daddy whistling in front, all our friends out on the sidewalk, crying and waving. I begged Daddy to let me go back, but he said that he had to follow the moving van. My lost world.

I sat crying in the backseat, looking out at the changing world around us. Facing blocks of apartment buildings, then turning onto a tree-lined highway. And then what seemed like hours later, Daddy pulled into the driveway of a big gray house, he and Mommy laughing as they told me and Richie to get out. "We're home, boys!"

Home. Our new home. Not as big as the one I remembered in Japan, or the other one where I lived with my other parents, but way bigger than our four-room apartment. A finished basement with a playroom and boiler room that Daddy, an amateur photographer, turned into a darkroom. A whole new world that I loved to explore, leaving my body to wander the house upside down, my back to the ceiling, going up and down the stairs, looking down at the carpeted floors. A big house with a big attic that had a closet I liked to hide in, not consciously remembering the past life you'll hear about later. But when I was a little older and learned about Anne Frank, I'd hide there, pretending to be her. On the ground floor, a big long living room, dining room, den, a long kitchen in the back, a little bathroom, and upstairs three bedrooms, one for me and Richie, one for Mommy and Daddy – no more sleeping in the living room – and a guest room for family and friends to stay in when they came to visit.

I made a new best friend there, Janie Dworman, who's still in my life. Janie took me walking in the woods behind our house and taught me about mushrooms, berries, frogs, salamanders, turtles, and rocks, which she introduced me to as "green quartz," "brown quartz, "red quartz," and "yellow quartz." We played in the mud, dug holes, and as evening fell, Janie introduced me to fireflies, which I'd never seen before. And as that first summer slowly ended, Janie taught me what to look for – green leaves turning brown, brown falling down – all of that grounded in what I'd learned from Grandpa. Amber, umber, golden leaves falling. Then sitting on the window seat watching the snow falling on our front lawn. Covering it. Blanketing over the bushes. Etching the trees in white. Bundled up in sweaters. The radiators hissing. And at night another fire in the fireplace.

I was playing upstairs one morning when I heard Mommy calling my name. Was I in trouble? I couldn't tell from the sound of her voice. Running downstairs, I followed her voice into the den. At the far end, on the same old couch we had in our apartment, Mommy was kneeling with her back to me. She turned and said, "Come look." There was frost on the windows and she'd wiped a little clear circle in front of her. Then she wiped a second lower circle so that I could look out too, as I climbed up on the couch beside her. She pointed at the circle, pointed down. I followed her finger. And there, poking its golden head up through the snow – was a bright yellow point of something growing. "What is it Mommy?" She turned to me, smiling. "A crocus. The very first crocus. Telling us that spring is coming." Crocus. A word I never heard before.

So we knelt there, together. And in those few moments, my right eye, the eye closest to her – my right eye fully opened – fully opened to the world for the very first time. Thank you, Mommy! I'm still looking at flowers, all these many years later.

CHAPTER 12

My First Revelation

IN THE FAR CORNER of our backyard was a big old tree that everyone called "The Indian Tree." It had been planted long before by the natives of the area from one sapling poked through a hole in the center of another one, its growing branches staked so that they pointed off in two directions of a long-vanished fork in a trail. From time to time anthropologists would come to visit it, as it was one of the very last ones still standing on Long Island. I loved how its two huge branches looked, all covered with snow, and I loved the bushes on either side of it, all covered in snow too. New words to learn – rhododendron, hydrangea. And I loved the way that Summer had become Autumn, which became Winter, which was slowly changing – again!

One perfect warm afternoon during my first Spring in our new home, Janie and I were sprawled on the warm ground behind our garage, beneath a tangle of honeysuckle vines pouring over an old wood fence, with hundreds of bees diving in and out of them, circling, buzzing, around and above us. I was a bit tense, but Janie turned to me and said, "You don't need to be afraid of them. They're more interested in the flowers than they are in us." And I relaxed.

I'd never seen honeysuckle in bloom before and Janie showed me how to pick a yellow blossom, nip off the tiny green tip with my teeth, and then suck out the sweet nectar. Long arms of sunlight were angling down through the trees. And the warm earth, and the fragrance of the blossoms, and the bees swarming above us, humming as they darted in and out of those blossoms, shifted me, unhinged me. And I knew, in every one of my cells, that just as the bees tracked scent through air to find those blossoms, going back to the source of all that sweetness – I knew that Janie and I, the bees and blossoms, the vine, fence, yard, world, sun, all tracked back to an ultimate Source.

○

It didn't occur to me until years later that that Source might be what some people call God, a word that I hadn't learned yet, except for after someone sneezed and someone else would say, "God bless you!" And it was only looking back on it years later, when I was a student in college, that I realized that those luminous magical moments lying on our backs on the warm spring earth next to Janie Dworman – had been the very first of my major spiritual experiences, my first revelation.

CHAPTER 13

A Tale of Joy and Terror

WHEN I WAS AROUND EIGHT, not long before he left home, Dad took me into the city to the Metropolitan Museum of Art. As mentioned in earlier stories, most of the time my relationship with him was awkward. I didn't enjoy playing catch with him, or basketball, the way that Richie did, but I loved our adventures on the Long Island Railroad, in the subway, and found common ground with him in the museums and art galleries he took me to. Wandering through large rooms filled with other people, we'd stop to admire and talk about paintings we liked, and sometimes to talk about paintings that we didn't like.

We'd gone to see a specific show, but I don't remember what it was. After walking through it we continued to wander through the museum and entered a large crowded room with a huge painting across from us of a young woman holding onto the branch of a small tree beside her, staring out into space. There were three shadowy figures floating in the trees behind her, who she was clearly listening to. I said nothing to my father for a long time, then asked, "Who is she?" He answered, "Joan of Arc." I didn't know who she was, but for the first time in my life I knew that I wasn't the only one who heard voices. Joy coursed through my body and for the next three days I was in heaven, knowing that someone else, a woman named Joan, had heard voices too.

My father was a moody man, a brooding man, and early on I learned not to ask questions, or I'd be shamed. "What do you mean you don't know who Joan of Arc is!? Everyone knows about her!" But slowly over time I came up with a tactic to use in such situations, and three days later I turned to him. "Daddy, I forget. Who was that lady in the painting?" He told me again that her name was Joan of Arc and then told me the story of her life. Of her work and her mission and her capture. Then he told me about her being burned at the stake, and to this day I can feel in my body the horror that rose up in me! As past lives of torture and murder rose to the surface of my mind – for a terrifying instant! And then I forced them back down, out of my conscious brain, terrified that if I did what I came here to do – I would be killed again! This also spiraling into my little Jewish body, unconsciously, in the years not so long after the Holocaust, and into Nanny's horror and survival story.

○

I stopped leaving my body to explore the house, which was totally under my control, and slowly over time I discovered that if I sang songs very loudly and quickly in my head I could block out the voices, but there was nothing that I could do when they talked to me and recited poems while I was sleeping. (Later I'll tell you a story about one of those poems and what came from hearing it over and over again.) And there was nothing I could do to stop the short recurring dreams that I'd have every few months, triggered by seeing that painting:

I am an old man in a long white robe. I walk into a strange room whose ceiling is held up by strange columns. Diagonally across from me a young woman walks in, my daughter. I'm about to greet her when someone stabs me in the back. I wake up.

I'm standing in a big tent, with a bloody saw in my hand, above a man being held down on a table, whose shattered leg I've just removed, when a bomb falls on the horse-drawn cart just outside the entrance to the tent, and it explodes. I wake up.

I am sitting in a wheel chair looking down at my left leg, missing below the knee. I lift up a small loaded pistol and put it in my mouth. Then I wake up.

A single dream, never repeated. I'm in summer camp, around ten, asleep on the bottom bunk when the boy above me knocks his pillow down. In the instant it falls on my face I have an entire dream-memory of a life when I'm in hiding. Captured. Jailed. Tried. Found guilty. Led up to a guillotine and beheaded.

○

Sometimes over the years – this must be the fiction-writer in me – when I've told people this story, I add that after I asked my father who she was and he told me "Joan of Arc," I wondered if she was Noah's wife. Noah and the ark. But that isn't true. I made it up later. And a few years ago I learned that the 19th century French artist who painted that amazing painting – Jules Bastien-Lepage – was also a gay man! For years I've kept a framed postcard of the painting on my bookshelf.

○

While most of my recurring dreams were nightmares, I did have one fun dream again and again for years. I'm a young boy living on a different planet, learning how to drive. My teacher and I are humanish, but not Earthlings. He is seated beside me, helping me out, as the small triangular vehicle is powered by telepathy and I have to focus my mind to raise it and get it to fly. When I reached puberty in this life I had a fun expanded version of the dream. Kids on that planet were not raised by our parents but in collective homes, in pods of seven, eight, nine kids, all the same age. When it was time to take our driving test, we had to raise up a bigger triangular flying car using mind control, and fly over the city as the driving teacher instructed us, while all the other kids in our pod were in the open back of the car – naked and having wild sex like we'd do each night at home!

CHAPTER 14

Radical Transformation

GRANDMA DIED. THAT CHANGED everything, although I didn't know it at the time. Or, her death changed Daddy, and he changed everything. But not right away. I remember the morning when Mommy and Daddy sat me and Richie down to tell us she died. We'd just gotten up. They looked distraught, I was starting to cry, and being the sometimes-mean big brother that I was, I turned to Richie and said, "Why aren't you crying?"

In first grade my parents took me to see a therapist. They told me it was because of my temper tantrums. (Years later they told me it was because of my mother's fear about my being a little homosexual.) I remember my tantrums. Looking back, I can feel my parents' usually repressed anger, and how I was the one it often flowed out of. Each therapy session would start with me sitting in a room by myself, putting together a model boat or an airplane, while the therapist talked with my mother. I got bored one day and went into the next room, where he and Mommy were talking. He asked me to go back into the other room for a while, then he'd join me. As I turned around I saw that the mirror on *my* side of the door – was see-through glass on *his* side! I was outraged. Felt spied on. Refused to go back. And my parents didn't make me.

One good thing came out of my time with that therapist. Each week on the way to his office we passed a Christian religious shop. After several near-tantrums about it, Mommy agreed to let me buy the little grey-haired angel figurine that was sitting in the window. She refused to enter the store herself but gave me the money for it. It sat for many years on top of the bookshelf in my bedroom, next to a little statue of a cowboy that someone once gave me. I don't remember who.

At first Richie and I shared a bedroom, but at one point I insisted on moving into the guest room, and Mommy and Daddy let me. Most nights, while Mommy was downstairs doing the supper dishes, Daddy would tuck Richie in and then he and I would play on his and Mommy's bed, tickling each other, wrestling on the brown corduroy bedspread that Grandma made for it. One night, out of breath, lying side by side, propped up on our elbows, Daddy turned to me and said, "I won't be coming home anymore." I remember wailing, "No Daddy. No! No! No!" Pounding him on the chest. Begging him to not go. And I remember how he carried me into my bedroom, dumped me on my bed, sobbing, then closed the door, walked down the hall, and filled up the bathtub.

At some point I fell asleep and Mommy came to wake me in the morning and asked me to come into Richie's room, where she woke him up and told us that Daddy wouldn't be coming home any more. And then she listed all the ways in which our lives would change. No new clothing for me. Just Richie. I was always the same size as our older cousins Larry and Michael so I would get their hand-me-downs. But Richie was shorter and she would only be able to afford to buy one of us new clothes. Although she did promise me one new outfit a year. But nothing to the dry cleaner, and no weekly visits from Sam the seltzer man. On and on. But that's not the story that I want to tell you now.

Like his mother, Daddy didn't like animals, and one of the very first things we did after he left was to get ourselves a dog. I paid for her, and still have the faded receipt. $5.00. My entire allowance savings. She was a crazy beagle I named Taffy. And most of what I know about love, I learned from her. The two of us going for endless walks in Hempstead Lake State Park, a few blocks from our house, after what we called "the backwoods" behind our house was divided up and eight houses were built there. Taffy and me kicking our way through fallen leaves. Watching other kids on their sleds and toboggans, playing games with each other, as we slowly walked around the lake, Taffy with her nose to the ground, me with my eyes in the trees.

I grew up with books all around me and I was read to every night by my parents, and Irmgard my second mother was always giving me books, one of which, *Nobody's Boy* by Hector Malot, is one of the books I've read and reread the most in my life. Irmgard was one of my mother's best friends, lost most of her friends and family in the Holocaust, never married, and took care of me so well after my father left. So books and stories, yes – but my favorite hobby was drawing and painting. I was the class artist. The one who made all the Christmas decorations for the windows of our classroom and for the hallways of the school. The one who drew and painted and played with clay. My art and my smarts and my bee-love the only thing that kept this little sissy boy from being endlessly made fun of. Even the toughest boys, when they came to play baseball in our backyard with my brother, would run away when the bees came out of their hive in the hole in the middle of the Indian Tree, while I would stand there calmly and let them walk all over me.

My kindergarten teacher Florence Countryman made me fall in love with learning, a gift which nourishes me to this very day. And one afternoon my third grade teacher Jeanette Winetsky stood in front of the class, just to the side of her desk, opened up a hard-bound book, and started to read to us, slowly, a poem.

Words began to come at me. Enter me. Dance. Sway. Rearrange me. Energize me. Mesmerize me. Hypnotize me. Vivify me. Mrs. Winetsky's warm voice. The silence in the room as she read. Sounds rising up. Filling the room. Filling my body. Dancing. Entrancing. Enhancing:

> the jingling and the tinkling...
> the rhyming and the chiming...
> the clamor and the clangor...
> Of the bells, bells, bells, bells—
> Bells, bells, bells –
> To the moaning and the groaning of the bells.

My entire body was trembling as Mrs. Winetsky stood in front of our third grade class and looked up from her book, closed it, and in her warm and caring teacher's voice said, "The poem that I just read you was written by Edgar Allen Poe and it's called 'The Bells.'" I'd never heard of him before, and I'd never heard anyone do anything with sound, with words, the way that Poe did. Utterly changed, seduced, enamored, I, the class artist, went home that afternoon and wrote my very first poem. And I've been writing ever since.

○

Many years later I came upon these words of Emily Dickinson written in a letter to T. W. Higginson in 1870: "If I feel physically as if the top of my head were taken off, I know that is poetry." – and that's rather like what happened to me the day Mrs. Winetsky read to us – but instead of the top of my head being taken off – hearing Poe's poem put the aching grieving fractured-family top of my head back on the rest of my damaged little frightened skull. And it was only years later that I understood that my misadventure with therapy led me to create my very first meditation altar – an angel and a cowboy standing next to each other on the top of the bookcase next to my bed – years and years before George Michael's 1991 song "Cowboys and Angels."

○

Thank you Irmgard for *Nobody's Boy!* The other books I've read again and again are *Crow Boy* by Taro Yashima, *Madeline* by Ludwig Bemelmans, *The Phantom Tollbooth* by Norton Juster, *The Decline and Fall of Practically Everybody* by Will Cuppy, *The Kin of Ata Are Waiting for You* by Dorothy Bryant, *To the Lighthouse* and *Mrs. Dalloway* by Virginia Woolf, *The Blue Estuaries* by Louise Bogan, and *Journal of a Solitude* and *Mrs. Stevens Hears the Mermaids Singing* by May Sarton, the second of which I've been reading again as I've been tinkering with this book. I repeatedly wander through a collection of Emily Dickinson's poems, and over the years I've composed songs for about ten of them, but I can't say that I've ever read it from cover to cover. The reference book I've gone back to over and over again since Dad and I first discovered it in the Eight Street Book Store in Greenwich Village when I was in high school is *A Dictionary of Angels* by Gustav Davidson.

Like standing at the food bar in your favorite restaurant, about to serve yourself your favorite treats, reading these books over and over again has fed my soul and shaped my life and the stories that you've been reading.

CHAPTER 15

More Radical Transformation

IT WAS SEPTEMBER OF 1960, the first day of fourth grade. I can still see where I was sitting in Mrs. Pearl Goldman's class as she passed out our new books. Math, English, Science, Social Studies. A pile in front of each of us on our small wooden desks, desks old enough to still have a small round hole in the upper right hand corner, from the days when kids wrote with a pen dipped into a bottle of ink, that hole where you put your ink bottle, always in the upper right hand corner, in the days when all lefties had to learn to write with their right hand.

The first day of fourth grade. Sitting toward the back of the room, on the leftish side when facing forward, a row in from the windows.

A sunny day. The first day of fourth grade. Sitting in my wooden chair at my wood-topped desk with a hole in the upper right corner. A pile of new textbooks stacked up in front of me.

Mrs. Goldman is talking as she walks around our sunny classroom passing out our new books. Us being around twenty-five students. She is walking and talking and passing out books and I'm sitting at my desk looking through them. Math. Science. English. Social Studies. I'm sitting at my desk on a sunny day in September, beginning to flip through the pages of my Social Studies book. My favorite subject.

Flip. Flip. Pages turning. Then my new book falls open in front of me near the beginning, and in the upper left-hand corner of a page – there's a drawing in black and white, about two inches wide and two inches high – the rendering of a room. I read the words below the drawing. "A home in ancient Egypt."

Ancient Egypt! A place I'd never thought about before, read about before, except in Hebrew School, where Richie and I went two afternoons a week and on Sunday. And from the stories we read and were told at Passover Seders.

Ancient Egypt. I fall into the drawing. Walk into that room, that room with its fat columns that are rounded on the bottom, nothing like the Greek or Roman-inspired columns in the neo-classical buildings all around us. No. Fat. Round at the bottom. Just like the ones in my most recurring dream, of being an old man who walks into a large room with strange columns holding up the ceiling, who's stabbed in the back and dies, just as my lovely daughter walks into the room from a door across from me. I fall into that beautiful drawing of a very familiar room, rather like my experience of going to see the Japanese house. I look down at that amazing drawing in my new Social Studies book and read the caption again: "A home in ancient Egypt."

○

When I told Mommy about learning about ancient Egypt in school and really liking it, leaving out of course any mention of my dream – she got very upset. Egypt, she told me, is where our ancestors were enslaved. I knew that, from all those Passover stories, but this felt different. And it was the early 1960s and my mother told me about contemporary Egypt and the still-new State of Israel, and how the people of Egypt want to destroy our people again. And I thought but didn't say, "Mommy, you're confusing things," and never talked about Egypt with her again.

When I told Daddy about learning about ancient Egypt in school and really liking it – on weekends when Richie stayed home and I went into the city by myself to spend the weekend with him and his second wife Pat, he'd take me to museums to see anything that had to do with Egypt. We wandered through vast rooms filled with Egyptian artifacts, and paintings, and sculpture, he bought me all kinds of books on ancient Egypt, which I never showed to Mommy. One of them was on Egyptian hieroglyphics, which I started to teach myself to read and write, and my readings led me to fall in love with the 18th Dynasty and Pharaoh Akhenaton, Queen Nefertiti, his monotheistic experiment, and his follower King Tut. And I became a new person. A new boy. A whole new boy who knew that he's part an old man who lived thousands of years before. And that little old man-boy was happy in a whole new way. Grounded. Expanded. Present and excited about learning even more.

○

After seeing the drawing in my new Social Studies book of that beautiful house in ancient Egypt – I never had that dream about it again!

CHAPTER 16

My First Visitation

THIRD GRADE - BELLS. Fourth grade – Egypt. Fifth grade – this story.

One day I came home from school and found my cousin Eileen in our backyard, playing on the swings. As soon as they saw me, Mom and Aunt Myra, Eileen's mom, came out and told me that Nanny was in the hospital. She'd had a stroke and was in a coma. They wouldn't let me or Richie or Eileen go to see her, and she died two weeks later. They wouldn't let us go to the funeral either – we were too little.

When Grandma died I was sad, but she scared me. When Nanny died I was devastated. She was the one who held me and my life together after Dad left, after Mom had to go to work. Nanny taught me how to cook, continued to read and tell me stories, and offered a continuity that kept me from totally falling apart. Nanny and her plants. Nanny and her magical garden. Nanny and her closet of beads I loved to string. Nanny and her tea and cookies. I still had some wrapped in white paper napkins in a glass casserole dish in the kitchen, and I'd go and smell but not eat them, wanting to keep them forever.

About two weeks after Nanny died I got in bed one night, the light still on beside my bed, and reached over to the bookcase the lamp sat on to grab the Hardy Boys book that I was reading. I don't remember which. Maybe *The Clue in the Embers*. As I reached for the book, picked it up in my left hand, and turned back and leaned into the pillow I'd placed up against the wall – Nanny appeared at the foot of my bed.

In movies ghosts are often see-through shapes of who they used to be, but Nanny was as solid in death as she had been in life. Only – she was sixty-four when she died but she looked to be around forty as she stood there, gazing at me. Younger than I ever knew her. She was wearing a big silvery shimmery hat with a wide brim and a very fancy elegant silvery outfit and a beautiful string of beads around her neck, none of which she could ever have afforded in life.

Standing about two feet from the foot of my bed, Nanny looked down at me and said, "Always remember that we belong to the bear clan." Then – she vanished.

"Always remember that we belong to the bear clan." I had no idea what that meant, and sat with my back against the wall, stunned, grateful, and in a state of blessed amazement. Knowing that it wasn't easy for her to do, but that she got all dressed up and came all the way to my bedroom to apologize to me for having told me that there is no God and that when you die they bury you in the ground and you rot away.

○

Now fast-forward about thirty years. It's the 1970s. I'm out of college, living in Park Slope, Brooklyn, working in The Community Bookstore, which is still there. Writing, and meditating, exploring different spiritual traditions, and taking a class with a Native American teacher. He was Pueblo. I can't remember his name. But after one of our first classes I approached him when everyone else was gone and told him the story about Nanny coming to visit me.

"Bear Medicine is powerful. Because of the way that they hibernate, my people see them as standing at the gateway between worlds and we call them the guardians of Dream Time."

I've been writing my dreams down for years, and was in and led dream groups with my dear friend Barbara Shor for many years. And for years I've kept a small black metal bear on the shelf in my bedroom closet in front of the framed pictures of my ancestors – parents, grandparents, great grandparents, which you've heard about already.

CHAPTER 17

Good-bye and Hello

I HAD ALMOST NO FRIENDS. Spent almost all my afternoons by myself in the public library. At some point in fifth or sixth grade someone gave me a book of Greek myths and I fell in love with Greek mythology and read everything on the subject I could find!

Our house was falling down around us and the yard was a mess. Mom couldn't afford the house, or to pay a gardener, as most of our neighbors did, and with little or no support from my father, she sold the house and moved us into a little apartment right across the street from what people called "the wrong side of town." When you're in your first year of high school and you used to live in a big house with the right address, things like that are very difficult.

Having entered puberty, my fascination was with other boys, which added to my sense of being a mistake. I'd rush home from school to take a shower in the bathroom I had to share with my brother and jerk off under the hot water spray, thinking of one sexy boy or another from school. Not long after we moved there I was diagnosed with a duodenal ulcer, and the muscles in the bottoms of my feet stopped growing, although my feet didn't and came to resemble two tightly drawn bows, with toes and heels pulled together. I hobbled about with special shoes and metal plates inside them, and had to have all kinds of different treatments. By age fifteen I was a wreck, waking from horrible nightmares almost every single night, usually of being abducted by aliens. Our full-time working Mom sleeping in the smaller bedroom next to ours, in our little ground floor apartment on the edge of the wrong side of town.

At the time I was fascinated with Japanese culture and decided that I was going to commit suicide by disemboweling myself – in the bathtub. Not wanting to make too much of a mess I began to save the plastic bags that dry-cleaned clothing comes in. But since I never wore anything that had to be dry-cleaned like Mom and Richie did, since all of my clothing was hand-me-downs, I'd sneak them out of Mom's closet but never from Richie's, knowing he'd notice. I hid the garment bags in a red plaid suitcase in the back of my side of the closet that Richie and I shared, a suitcase Nanny had given me, intending to tape those plastic bags over all the tiles and the stall shower doors before I killed myself, making it so much easier to clean up – never once thinking about how Mom or Richie would feel when they found me. (That little detail should tell you something about what a mess I was.)

I measured out how many plastic bags I would need, and one Tuesday or Wednesday I realized that I had enough of them, and so I planned to kill myself that Friday. I was home from school that afternoon and Richie was out playing with friends. I remember sitting at my desk, struggling with my math homework and slamming a pencil into the Formica fake-wood top of my desk and breaking it. Math was my worst subject. Then I realized it didn't matter anymore if I finished it, because I was going to be dead in a few days, and turned back to my homework – when the light in the room changed. The late afternoon sun had been streaming through the open Venetian blinds to my right – then it wasn't. We lived on the ground floor and I assumed that a large truck had parked on the street and was blocking the light. But when I turned to look – standing to my side about three feet away – solid, blocking the light – was a humanish being with blue skin and short pointy ears that hung down like a dog's. He was looking right at me with his deep dark eyes, and to this day when I try to describe him I always say that he was neither naked nor clothed, as if there were a protective covering over him that was also a part of him, perhaps like hide... but not quite. And I call him a him, because I don't know what other pronoun to use. He was a him, but a very different him than a human Earth him.

For about ten seconds he stood there, beaming at me what I can only, in retrospect, describe as love. And then – he vanished – taking with him any thought I had about putting an end to my life! And taking with him – any thought or memory I might have had about his visit! Yes, that vanished too. Completely. And from that moment all my nightmares stopped too, and have never come back.

○

Some time later my mother met Merl, who became her second husband. There was a day some years later when, in a drunken rage, he grabbed me from behind and would have choked me to death – I was blacking out – but Mom walked in suddenly, screamed, and he dropped me on the floor. But that's a whole other story for a whole other book.

Anyway, Merl Shields lived in California and we were packing up to move there. I remember sitting in front of my closet, pulling out my old red suitcase, unzipping it – and a huge wad of plastic dry-cleaning bags burst out of it! For an instant I was filled with rage, sure that Richie had stuffed them in there. And then – I remembered!

We moved when I was in my late teens. For the next ten years my memory of that blue visitor would surface and disappear again from my conscious mind. A decade later, he returned to my life again, as one of the beings I was channeling. I thought that he would be able to fill me in on my abduction nightmares but what he told me was more startling than anything I could have imagined. He said that he had been with me in spirit on the planet I lived on before I came to Earth. All at once my terror of aliens flipped around, and I began to open up to my own reawakened memories – of being an alien myself!

CHAPTER 18

With New Eyes

MOM MARRIED MERL IN Aunt Myra's living room. The next day we flew to Florida to visit my mother's father and his wife, and then we flew to Los Angeles. My new stepbrother Roger met us at the airport and drove us to our new home, in Los Alamitos, in Orange County. It was January and had been bitterly cold in New York, but we were in a whole new world. Outside my bedroom window was a line of night-blooming jasmine bushes, intoxicating as I lay in bed that night with the windows wide open. A flower I'd never heard of before, with a heavenly smell that I'd never smelled before!

When we moved to California I was reborn. People say you take your problems with you. I did. But they looked very different next to cactuses and under palm trees than they had next to azaleas and under maples. For the first time I had a group of friends, a few of whom are still in my life. Alas, there were kids who hated me because I was Jewish, which I'd grown up hearing about but never experienced, blocking my path on the way to class with their taunts – "You killed Christ!" or shouting at me – "Your God is the God of anger, and our God is the God of love!" Or from the slightly kinder kids – "What happened to your horns?" – "What side of your pants do you wear your tail on?" Always coming from boys and never girls – which made me feel proud to be a Jew, and that pride supported me later, when I was ready to come out as gay.

Merl had a sister Nubs who lived in Tucson, and not long after we moved there her husband Hank was diagnosed with bone cancer which had spread, and we drove out to see them. I was an opinionated high school boy, quiet in school but not at home, and I remember saying on the drive there that with so many people starving around the world, we shouldn't try to keep dying people alive as they were working to do with Hank.

Hank and Nubs lived in a small trailer out in the desert, another new alien world for me. I remember our first meal. It was hot. We were sitting around a little table, Mom and Merl, my brother and me, with Hank sitting in a wheelchair to my left. He was emaciated, and one side of his jaw had been removed. Nubs was at the stove, cooking, bringing things to the table, and everyone was talking as I sat silently beside Hank, sometimes staring at him out of the corner of my eye, fascinated, and then turning away, repelled.

Nubs brought over a bowl of bright green guacamole, which was new to me – we never had it in New York. In fact, I'd never heard of avocadoes till we moved. As everyone was talking, a large bright green fly flew in and began to circle the bowl. Two different greens. One dark. One iridescent. Mom and Merl kept swatting it away, but it kept buzzing back. And then I turned to look at Hank – and his eyes were following that huge green fly that kept diving down into the big bowl of bright green guacamole that was starting to turn a bit black along the edges. He was following that big loud green fly with his eyes – with a look of joy on his face that I had never seen before – a look of joy and bliss and pleasure – at just simply being alive in his old worn cut-up body – a look of ecstasy on his sliced-apart face that I had never seen before. I kept staring at Hank, his joy at being alive thoroughly infectious, and I began to feel more alive than I'd felt since I was a very little boy. Thank you Uncle Hank!

○

On the way home, sitting in the back seat of the car, I told Mom and Merl what had happened to me from watching Hank, said that I was wrong, made my amends to them for what I had said, and was very sad that he died soon after and I never got to be with him again.

PART 2

On My Own

CHAPTER 19

Molecular Affirmation

I GRADUATED FROM Western High School in Anaheim in June of 1969 and went off to U. C. Santa Barbara in the fall. What quirk of fate assigned me as a roommate Erick Faigin, another Jewish boy, one of three of us in our dorm? There was nowhere on our applications that we had to put down our religion. He had dark curly hair and was the first boy I knew who already had a beard and a mustache, in addition to a full set of braces on his teeth – when most kids get them in junior high. He was very proud of his little red VW bug. I didn't drive at all. Vision-impaired. And there was never a single book I mentioned that he hadn't already read, and he believed that some music is holy but other music isn't. If a holy record was playing on his little stereo – Joni Mitchell or Laura Nyro – and it was time to go to class – we had to leave the record playing in our absence till it finished. But if a record wasn't holy – say, Bob Dylan – we could lift up the arm, stop it from playing, and turn off the stereo, which lived on the top of the dresser in his closet.

Erick's first gift to me was a copy of *Siddhartha* by Herman Hesse, who I'd never heard of before – and I loved it! He told me that I should be a Religious Studies major and not an Anthropology major, and guided me to take classes with him in Hinduism and Buddhism. And Erick was the person who taught me the word that I'd been seeking – "spirituality." As in, "Hey Andy, you're on a spiritual path. You just don't realize it." And he persuaded me to take a Religious Studies class with a professor who encouraged us to trust our instincts, which was something no one had ever suggested to me and which I interpreted as: "Trust your inner voices."

Around that time I would walk through the stacks in the library – and books would literally fall off the shelves at my feet. One, on reincarnation, which I checked out, taught me that the places I remembered from as far back as age three were from my past lives. Another time Jack London's amazing book *Star Rover* fell off a shelf right at my feet, which is also about reincarnation. In the same way I read books on healing, mysticism, and a fascinating book with a deep purple cover about Chinese eunuchs – all of which clued me into parts of my greater self.

One evening I went by myself to see a born-again Christian hippie version of Samuel Beckett's play *Waiting for Godot*. It was all about sacrifice, pain, surrender, suffering, and a character was chanting over and over again, "Singing, burning, singing, burning." I didn't want to be there but sat, miserable, until a very loud male voice in my head said: "Go. To stay would be death for you." So I got up and left, which was so not like me, to wander the campus at night, wondering who and what the voice was.

There was a cute boy down the hall named Norm who became my guide to marijuana and other substances, which I'd never tried before, but which Erick had no interest in. One day I went down the hall to his room and he opened the door, all excited, and told me that someone had just given him two hits of LSD, and reached out to hand me a tab. As I extended my hand a very clear voice said to me, "Do not do this until your fortieth birthday." I didn't take it, told Norm, "I'm not supposed to do this till my fortieth birthday," and went back to our room to hang out with Erick.

Another time I was walking by myself on the bluff above the ocean, wandering by the edge of the slough. All at once everything around me shifted. The slough became a small stream, the beach looked different, and for about three seconds I could see a group of Native American men in buckskins, dancing together in a circle. Then everything went back to normal and I continued walking. But I didn't tell anyone about it, not even Erick. In his presence, I wanted to appear normal and in control.

The struggle I was in with myself had two parts. One was the conflict between having a spiritual focus and a political focus, which went back to the tension between my maternal and paternal lineages. But deeper than that my major question was whether or not someone, "me," could become what I called "A Real Person." When I brought it up one night with Erick, lying in the dark in our parallel beds – he knew exactly what I was talking about! "Is it possible to be a real person? Is it possible for a person to live an open honest authentic life?" We had no evidence that it was, two boys from broken homes with difficult damaged parents and stepparents, but we were excited by the possibility of there being such a person and kept talking about it.

Erick and I took the same classes. Ate together. Double-dated with our girlfriends. Went to rallies and marches and protests together. One day he came back to our room and announced that a swami was going to be speaking on campus and said that I had to go with him. Given my inner shifts you'd think I'd be interested, but I said no, remembering a TV episode from, I think, an old *Abbott and Costello* show, that had a phony swami in it. But Erick insisted. Persisted. Till I finally gave in. But I was furious. Even more so because there was a holy album on and we had to let it keep playing. And the moment we stepped in the hall and I locked the door, as we were heading toward the stairs, Erick stopped and said, "I have to go back and get my cup," a tin cup that he always took with him. I was pissed. Said we didn't have time. That if we were going to go, we shouldn't be late. Erick insisted. I relented and he went back to get it. And then we ran to the other side of campus to the lecture hall.

I always liked to sit in the back row, where I could hide, but Erick always sat in the front row, where he could ask questions about things he didn't follow. Not only did I hate to sit in front, but I hated to sit next to him, and we stood in the back of the lecture hall, bickering. As always, he won, and we sat in the front row. A few moments later a dark-skinned man entered the lecture hall by himself, but instead of taking the chair behind the table in front of the room or standing behind the lectern beside it, he pulled himself up on the table and crossed his legs. Then he looked down at us and said, "I'm very thirsty. Is there a water fountain nearby?" Erick looked up at the swami and said there was, but a new building was going up and due to a recent rain everything was muddy and it would be hard to get to the water fountain. But, he said, "I have a cup. I'll go fill it up."

The two of us walked over wooden planks, through mud, Erick filled up his metal cup, we went back and he handed it to the swami. The room had gotten noisy as other students had arrived. I can't remember if someone introduced the swami. What I do remember, fifty-five years later, is how he began his talk. "If you are living in harmony with the universe, everything will work out. For example, I was thirsty and turned to these two young men and asked them where I could find a water fountain. One of them said, 'I have a cup.'" I believe he held up the cup. I have a clear sense of his hands. Of brown fingers that seemed to have an extra joint, they were so long. A thumb that lay flat in the middle of his palm. Perfectly opposable, as if it emerged from his wrist. That's all I remember of the swami's talk. Not one single other word.

Erick at I looked at each other, sitting side by side, he on my left, in the seat by the center aisle, and we knew what the other one was thinking. "Yes. Yes. Yes. It *is* possible to be a real person!" Although neither of us had ever seen "a real person" before, we both knew that we had just met one!

Erick's guidance and everything that had happened to me that year in Santa Barbara led up to those moments in that lecture hall, looking up at Swami Prabhavananda. Yes. In those moments the swami answered our question, and gave us all the information we needed in order to know that our inner work was working – by the feedback we'd get from the world.

○

A decade later I was in massage school and working in a bookstore in Greenwich Village. One day I was unpacking a carton and pulled out a new book by gay author Christopher Isherwood called *My Guru and his Disciple*. When I read the back cover I discovered that it was about Swami Prabhavananda, who founded the Vedanta Society in Los Angeles, where he taught from 1930 till he died in 1974. My first reaction was – "Jerk, you could have gone down to LA to study with him!" Of course I bought the book, but for months after reading it I was tormented by my lost opportunity – till I realized that he had given me all that I needed – in a few words and a single glance. That was my initiation. That was all I needed. And I took a solemn vow before God, then and there:

I will never leave the world.

I will have no living teacher.

I will find You on my own.

A decade or so after that, as I was moving toward my fortieth birthday, I became obsessed with the words I'd heard when Norm was about to give me a tab of LSD. "Do not do this until your fortieth birthday." Did that mean that I should do it? I spent several sessions talking about it with my therapist and decided that I did not *have* to take LSD, and so far, all these years later, I haven't. Although not having ever taken it has continued to dance in my head, as you will hear about later on.

CHAPTER 20

My Second Revelation

I REMEMBER A NIGHT near the end of the school year, when Erick and I tried out a new fad that boys were doing on campus. First, you get stoned out of your mind. We didn't. Then, you go to the laundry room with a friend and bundle yourself up in a blanket and get inside the clothes dryer. Erick wanted to try it. I didn't. I helped him wrap himself up. Helped him get into the big front-door dryer. Closed the door. Put the coins in. And it started, and he turned around. Loudly. Once. And I realized we hadn't come up with a signal for him to let me know when to stop. But by then we were so bonded that after one turn I opened the dryer door – to his great relief – dizzy – and helped him climb out.

Stars were shining as we crossed the grass. We could hear waves crashing on the beach below us, out of sight. Finals week was about to start. I remember saying, "Can you believe it? The school year was just beginning and now it's about to end. And soon we'll be graduating. And living out the rest of our lives. And soon we'll be dead!" We got through finals and went our separate ways for the summer, he to his family in Los Angeles, and me back East to stay with my father and stepfamily.

A week later I was in Maryland visiting my Brown cousins. We were sitting in the living room one night right after dinner when the phone rang. Bert went into the kitchen to get it, soon came back to say it was my mother, and told me to go into his and Joy's bedroom. I wanted to stay there with everyone, but he insisted, so I did. I was sitting on the edge of their bed, and I can still hear my mother saying, "I have very bad news. Erick was electrocuted." I was puzzled, unable to remember if electrocuted meant you were dead, or just badly shocked. And I had to ask. "Does that mean he's dead?" And she had to answer, "Yes."

Erick died at work, at his summer job in an aviation factory that his father got him, wanting to toughen him up. He'd told me all about it when we'd talked, a few nights before. How much he hated it. The boy who sometimes, every once in a while, occasionally, had told me that he might be a little bit attracted to other boys. Who was working with big burly men who kept *Playboy* pinups on the inside of their locker doors. Having nothing in common with them, during their lunch break Erick would go off by himself to read Kierkegaard and Nietzsche in a small room with a sign on the door that said, "Danger! High Voltage!" The coroner's report said he might have lived if he hadn't been wearing braces, which were due to be removed in two weeks. I can imagine him reaching out a fingertip to a row of fat electric cables running from floor to ceiling, maybe thinking about his adventure in the dryer, wanting to quickly touch the cables, wondering what it would feel like.

I flew back for the funeral. There's a photograph taken right after it, of a group of us standing behind his father and little half-brother at their kitchen table. I measure how out of touch I was with reality by that photograph. My best friend had just died, my teacher, my guide, and someone took out a camera, so I smiled. No one else did. Everyone else looks like you look after a funeral. Everyone but me.

After his funeral I flew back to New York for the rest of the summer, and spent some sad time in a hospital with my Aunt Myra, who was in a coma, then flew back to California to spend a week or so with my mom and brother and Merl. Then I went back to Santa Barbara for our, for my, sophomore year.

Erick and I were going to be living in single rooms side-by-side in a different dorm, up the hill above the lagoon. It was painful for me to be there, alone, with a stranger in what would have been his room. For days I wandered around that familiar beautiful campus in a state of shock, going to classes but not feeling present. Because we were inseparable, whenever I ran into someone the first thing they'd ask was – "Where's Erick?" And being a demented lunatic I'd answer – "Oh. He died," in the very same tone I would have used to say, "Oh. He transferred to UCLA."

He died. I lived. Signed up for classes. Spent comforting awkward time with my lovely girlfriend, tormented by the boys I fantasized about. Went, early in fall quarter, to change my major from Anthropology to Religious

Studies, as Erick had suggested. And I sat by the beach, meditating. Listening to the waves crashing. Watching the sexy surfer boys. Sat in my little single room with Erick not on the other side of the wall, reading books he'd already read, reading books he hadn't, books that I knew he would have loved too. Wondering how he could be gone when I was still there.

My first meditation teacher, Houston Wood, also changed my life in another way. Enamored of Hinduism, I said to him one day that I wanted to convert as he had. "Why would you want to do that when there's so much good stuff in your own tradition?" I had no idea what he was talking about, said so, and he told me about Kabbalah, about Jewish mysticism, and about the Jewish writings on reincarnation, *gilgul,* which no one in my family and none of my Hebrew school teachers had ever mentioned, and gave me a list of books to read, all of which I purchased and read, which changed my life, including *The Garden of Pomegranates* by Israel Regardi and *Nine Gates to the Chassidic Mysteries* by Jiri Langer, which are part of my archived papers. I'd gone to a Conservative Hebrew School, had a bar mitzvah, spent the following year with a group of boys meeting with our rabbi and reading Abraham Joshua Heschel, nothing of which I understood, and then I stepped out of any kind of formal Jewish life beyond Passover Seders and lighting Hanukkah candles – till Houston brought me back.

One afternoon I was walking up the hill by the lagoon on my way to my dorm after his class. As I got to the top a flock of crows landed in front of me and I thought – "Aunt Myra is dead!" When I entered the hallway I could hear my phone ringing through the door. I opened it, dashed in, grabbed the phone, and heard Mom's voice cracking. "Aunt Myra is gone," she said. "I know," I said, and told her about the crows.

One afternoon I was standing at the edge of the lagoon, in my favorite spot, grass under my feet, looking out to the sky. I was silent the way Grandpa taught me to be, and yet focused in a way that I'd learned from Houston. I wasn't thinking any particular thoughts. I wasn't looking for or expecting anything to happen. "Seek and ye shall find," Jesus said. For me, it was a case of seek and ye shall be found. Suddenly, something came down from the blue blue sky above me – a twenty foot long silvery cone of light – which penetrated my entire body. And for about ten seconds, ten very long slow timeless seconds, in that infinity of silence – I knew and saw and felt and was united with and understood, absolutely Everything! If you'd been standing beside me and asked how much water was in the Pacific Ocean – I could have told you, right to the gallon. And had you asked me how many grains of sand were on the beach – I would have given you the exact number.

Then the energy vanished and I was looking out over land, water, land, water, land, sky. Only, as I looked around me, I knew that I was radically transformed. The cone when it vanished took with it all the wisdom that it had shared with me. But it left me with a sense of serenity, a feeling of grace, and the total utter certainty that although all of that wisdom had vanished, leaving me as I had been before it arrived, that there was one thing that was utterly different – that for about ten seconds I had known Everything. God, and everything about God. The universe and every star, planet and virus. As if I were looking at a vast map. As if I had just read the trillion-volume *Encyclopedia of Absolutely Everything*. I knew why God created the universe, how it would unfold, and I knew exactly where it was going. And then, a moment later, all that I knew is that I knew all of that – just a moment ago.

Revelation. First, beneath honeysuckle – and then beside the lagoon.

CHAPTER 21

Yet More Radical Transformation

I SPENT MY JUNIOR YEAR abroad at Hebrew University in Jerusalem. While I didn't get a dorm-mate like Erick, I lived in a collective house for a while and then shared an apartment, and two of the men I lived with, Steve and Michael, have remained dear friends to this very day, more than fifty years later.

I met Michael soon after I arrived, on a camping trip to see the sunrise from a mountain called Sinai. I remember our slow climb to the top, ascending as the sky lightened. At the top, with no forethought, I fell to my knees and lowered my forehead to the ground – only to be taunted by a group of five or six young men around my age in Israeli army uniforms calling out – "Hey Ah-mose! Hey Ah-mose!" I have no idea why they chose Amos from all the prophets in the Bible, but it comically echoed back a TV comedy show I loved watching when I was a boy, called *Amos 'n' Andy!* And, the p-word.

While I loved living in Jerusalem, my time there turned me into an anti/post/non-Zionist, but that's another story for another time. And while I loved being at the university, it took some time to get used to the way things worked there. Being the odd character that I am, and given the cultural ripples washing through me – I took a class on Chinese art and culture. The professor, Dr. Irene Eber, was a short slim woman in her fifties with a heavy fascinating accent I couldn't place and sometimes had trouble understanding. In the first class she showed us a series of slides of Chinese landscape paintings, which I already loved, and told us something I didn't know – that each painting is a visual meditation where you start on the ground at the bottom left, wander through the landscape, breathing and opening yourself to the world, and then slowly ascend to the open sky in the upper left hand corner – which is Nirvana!

At the very end of our first class, as the forty or so of us were heading toward the door, Professor Eber made a beeline right to me. "Do you know that you're Italian?" I did, and said so. When I asked her how she knew that she told me that she'd lived in a town in Poland where the richest Jewish family were the Padukers, whose ancestors came from Padua in Italy, and that my last name meant "Roman," which Grandpa had told me just before my bar mitzvah. So, Roman, in Jerusalem, taking a class in Chinese art with an amazing woman with an utterly mysterious accent.

In the past I always sat in the back of a classroom. Somewhat following Erick's example, I didn't sit in the first row but in the middle, and when I came back the following week for our second class I sat up closer to the front and remained there.

One afternoon Dr. Eber said something, the context of which I can't remember at all, but given her heavy accent, none of us could understand what she said, which sounded something like: "The buhduh is the buhduh tree." We sat there puzzled, many of us American students, all of us knowing, in appropriate Israeli fashion, to not ask questions in class, but to hold on to them to ask the professor later during their office hours! But we were all curious and finally a young woman on the other side of the room timidly raised a hand. "I didn't understand what you just said, Professor." Dr. Eber repeated her words, a bit more slowly – "The buhduh is the buhduh tree." Again, none of us could understand what she said, and another brave young woman sitting closer to me repeated the same words the first student had said.

I remember how Dr. Eber shifted on her feet and then repeated her words, very very slowly, fully enunciating each syllable, emphasizing each sound, and exaggerating every vowel –

The bah'-dee is the boh'-dee tree.

Those words raced through me like a wind from nirvana. I was utterly transformed and sat in my seat literally trembling. Renewed, revived, reborn.

"The body – is the bodhi tree."

Back in third grade, when Mrs. Winetsky read us Edgar Allen Poe's poem "The Bells," she changed my life. Years later, when I came upon these words of Emily Dickinson: "If I feel physically as if the top of my head were taken off, I know that is poetry." – I knew that hearing Poe's poem had done the opposite – put the aching grieving fractured-family top of my head back on my damaged little skull.

That day in Irene Eber's class did something different. I was a smart wounded scared in-the-closet gay boy with a lovely girlfriend from Santa Barbara, but I had no connection to my body at all. If I could have lived as just a head, neck, right shoulder and right arm – I would have been perfectly content and entirely myself. And those words – "The body is the bodhi tree" – sent energy through my entire body and connected and en-livened me in a way that I had never felt before.

I sat there trembling. And I sat there, utterly transformed – for the rest of my life, to this very day. Embodied. In a holy Buddhist Chinese Jewish Polish way.

○

After class, clusters of us talked about what had happened and I discovered what I'd already suspected, that only two or three other students in our class knew what the bodhi tree was, but none of us were brave enough to ask Professor Eber another question.

I stayed in touch with Irene, who survived the Holocaust because neighbors hid her in their chicken coop for three years, in the town of Mielec. Most of her family died but if you saw the movie *Schindler's List*, her mother and sister survived because they worked for Schindler in his factory, and her curious accent came from the German and Yiddish of her childhood and the English she learned when she and her mother and sister made their way here after the war, all woven together with Hebrew.

We wrote letters back and forth and sometimes spoke on the phone, but never met again. One day on the phone I thanked her for changing my life and told her how her words began my journey of embodiment, which got me to massage school, to study shiatsu and other forms of bodywork, to become a body-centered therapist, called today a somatic therapist, and to have a practice doing that for a number of years in different clinics and independently. Irene asked me what she'd done to change my life, and when I told her the story she began to laugh more loudly than I'd ever heard her laugh before, and said, "There was a Buddhist master in China who had two wise students, but he didn't know which one should be his dharma heir, so he asked them both this question: 'What is the body, and what is the bodhi tree.' One student said, 'There is no body and there is no bodhi tree.' The other student said, 'The body is the bodhi tree,' and the master chose the first one to succeed him."

Then she started laughing again and I joined her. Because what changed my life for the way way better – was the losing answer! Irene did add that the losing student went on to found his own Buddhist lineage, and to this very day I can hear her words and what happened to me in her class that day, when she said them again slowly, and I and we were able to understand them. Me, a lover of trees to this very day. Grandpa, Nanny, Janie, Irene, and the trees.

CHAPTER 22

Good-bye and Hello Again

AUTHOR FLANNERY O'CONNOR WROTE in her book *A Prayer Journal*, "Oh Lord, I am saying at present I am a cheese; make me a mystic immediately!" But not me. I just wanted to be normal. Then I was living in Jerusalem, in a land with a long long history of prophets, and I remember a night walking home from class through the wadi beside the Monastery of the Cross, when a strong luminous male voice started talking to me about my being a prophet. An old familiar voice, long suppressed, repressed. The voice of God. To the amusement and horror of my housemates I built a large stone altar in our backyard. Our house was vegetarian, so I couldn't offer up animal parts, tried to burn lentils but couldn't figure out how to make them catch fire, so I started writing down the poems to God that would flow through me each morning, and then each evening I'd go out in the yard and burn them. But doing that didn't slow down or silence the voice, and I was getting more and more scared that I was crazy.

Once a week a fellow student a few years older than us, Selma Weiner, came to our house to teach us Rashi, the medieval rabbi and commentator. Her father was a noted Orthodox rabbi in New York, and if the Jewish world had been different back then she probably would have gone on to become a rabbi herself. The first time she came she was carrying two books – one that became our study guide, Rashi's Torah commentaries, and on top of it was a copy of D. H. Lawrence's book *Women in Love*. Intrigued and inspired, I bought a copy, devoured it, loved it, and a few weeks later Selma told us that a film-version was playing. Sitting in a matinee in an almost entirely empty theatre I came out to myself for the first time, not as gay, but as bi, when toward the end one of the characters says to her husband something like, "Aren't I enough for you as a woman?" and he answers something like, "You're enough for me as a woman, but I want an equal and opposite love with a man," that said soon after the death of his beloved male friend.

So, love and death, and voices. In books, films, and in my head.

The voice was getting louder and I was getting more and more scared. One day when Selma showed up for our weekly lesson all my housemates had other things to do, and I sat with her at our dining table, took a long slow breath, and told her about my voices. I'd never told anyone before, not even Erick. She smiled, didn't say, "I know a good psychiatrist," and gave me the name and number of a kabbalistic rabbi. I called and he invited me over.

Rabbi Fox was an American living in Jerusalem, an Orthodox rabbi whose first name, alas, I never knew. But he offered me some coffee as we sat in his book-lined study, asked me why I was there, and I told him. Everything. Going all the way back to my earliest years, just as I've told you.

What I was sure he'd say to me was, "Son, you seem like a very smart young man, but I'm afraid you have a very serious mental health problem, and I'd like to suggest that you see a good psychiatrist." Instead he looked at me, thoughtfully, and said, "In our tradition listening to voices is something that you should not do until you're forty, married, and living in the world in a stable way, with a good solid job."

So not what I expected. Forty, married, with a good job. I didn't say a thing about boys, we chatted for a while, I thanked him and returned home. And just as after the blue man visited me – from that afternoon on – I did not hear a single voice in my head again! A kind of miracle. For the first time in my life it was just me in my head. Okay, me and all the messages I'd been given about myself and about how to live in the world, by my parents, relatives, friends, and teachers. But for the first time it was just me and no other non-physical beings. Such a gift.

CHAPTER 23

Radical Redirection

I HAD FALLEN IN LOVE with Santa Barbara and being there changed my life, as you know. But three years later I was a different young man and during my time in Jerusalem I decided that I wanted to do my senior year at Berkeley. In a very different way, now older and more present in my body and in the world, I fell in love with Berkeley too. There wasn't a Jewish Studies program there yet, and Judaism was my focus, so as a Religious Studies major most of my classes were inter-departmental. I took a class my first quarter there with Professor Isaac Kikawada, a Japanese Episcopal priest who was an authority on Hebrew and all Semitic languages. Just as Irene was what I'll call a Westerner who had gone Eastern, Isaac was an Easterner who'd gone Western, and he became my second mentor.

One day Isaac came up to me as class was ending and said he wanted to talk with me. Nervous that I'd done something wrong, we chatted on our way to his office where he told me something like, "We're very impressed with the work you're doing here, and with what you've already studied. And there's a program here where you can get into a PhD program in your senior year." I was blown away. "And," he added, as the Vietnam War was still raging, "if you get in you can keep your student deferment." My draft lottery number was very low so I would probably have been drafted, as students lost their deferment when they got a BA. So I said yes. And there I was in my senior year in a PhD program, an underground one, Isaac told me, with a dissertation committee of three professors. In a very short time I had a dissertation topic – "North Syrian ivory carvings from the Second Millennia BC," which I'd fallen in love with during my year in Jerusalem when I worked as an archaeological assistant at the Israel Museum for an amazing man, an Italian Jew named Rudolf Cohen.

Always worried about me, my mother used to say, "You'll never survive in the real world. You'll have to get a PhD and live in an ivory tower somewhere." I had no idea what an ivory tower was, but there I was, in my senior year, a PhD student. My crazy amazing life unfolding before me.

After watching *Women in Love* I knew I had to deal with my attraction to other boys, men, and soon after I arrived in Berkeley I got into therapy. In our third session, when I was finally brave enough to tell her why I was there, Mary Auerswald said, in her strong Texas accent, "Darlin', I don't know anything about homosexuality, but if that's what you want to work on, then that's what we're gonna do!" I will always be grateful to her for the deep work that we did, and always be ashamed of how I treated my lovely girlfriend. But that too is another story, the short version of which is that I fell in love with a fellow student in the co-op I was living in, the first man/boy I ever kissed, a handsome outgoing fellow with a Palestinian mother and an Austrian father, the youngest of three boys, who grew up in South San Francisco. (If you're curious about where we met, go to Wikipedia and look up Barrington Hall.)

My time with him was wonderful, magical, and painful, as he liked having sex with other guys and found monogamously-inclined me to be way too possessive. But we lived together for a while, loved, danced, fought, broke up, got back together, played, went for long long walks, spent wonderful time with his parents, then broke up again – just around the same time after I graduated that governor Ronald Reagan heard about and gutted my PhD program, which had been created to keep rich white boys out of the draft, boys whose fathers were furious at Ronnie. Isaac explained it all to me, and said, long before anyone had invented the expression "gap year" – "Take a year off and then come back! You don't even have to apply. You're already in the program."

Distraught, a total wreck, with my next steps in love and life gone – my father and his partner Suzanne suggested that I come to visit them in New York and sent me a two-week round-trip ticket. I adored Suzanne from the day we first met in my freshman year, when I was still at Santa Barbara, and I adored her kids Evan and Kate. I loved cooking with her, talking with her, working with her in her gorgeous garden on the rooftop terrace. (Maybe you met her too. She was in several films and had a recurring part in the TV show *The Sopranos*. Look her up: Suzanne Shepherd.)

The second or third night that I was there she and I were sitting in the living room talking about my life, my ex-boyfriend, the PhD program, and she paused for a long time, nodded at me, and said – "Why are you doing this? You're a writer!"

All four of my parents knew that I wrote poems and stories, and all of them were writers themselves, but none of the other three ever said anything about my writing, or even asked about it.

"Why are you doing this? You're a writer!"

I called Isaac a few days later to tell him I wouldn't be coming back.

○

I like to say to people about that time in my life – "My father and step-mother sent me a 2-week round-trip ticket to New York, and I accidentally stayed there for 20 years."

But/and/so – "Why are you doing this? You're a writer!" – gave birth to all of my books, published and unpublished, and to the stories that you're reading. And Suzanne remained in my life till she died in November of 2023.

Thank you Momma. With love, always. The one who you called "My Andrey."

CHAPTER 24

My Second Visitation

ONE DAY DAD AND SUZANNE and Evan and Kate went off to the Metropolitan Museum of Art, but I wanted some alone time and decided to stay home. I was sitting on the terrace, surrounded by plants, looking out from the 12th floor over the buildings across from us on Broadway, out to Riverside Park, the Hudson River, and out to the Jersey Palisades in the distance.

It was a beautiful day. The sun was warm. I felt safe and comforted, sitting in an old metal chair, when I had the funny feeling you get when someone is staring at your back. I hadn't heard anyone come in, and turned around, expecting to see Dad, Suzanne, Kate, or Evan. Instead, Max, my Grandpa, was standing there, several months dead, a little taller than he was in life, dressed much nicer than he had ever dressed, in a tweed jacket, dark pants, a beige shirt and a V-neck sweater, looking younger than I knew him in life, just as Nanny had been when she appeared. And, unlike the traditional ghosts we know from movies, just like Nanny had been, and just like the blue man, Grandpa's body was as solid as if he were alive, blocking out the pots of cosmos and nasturtium behind him, and the little bust of Beethoven that hung above them on the brick wall. And somehow – music was pouring out of his body.

Struck by the music, I ran past him into the apartment, down the hall to the living room, and began to finger out the music on the piano. I can hear it to this day, and hear the words that went with it, which were a question and not a statement like Nanny's words had been, and somehow the words were from him to me, from him for me to give to him, and a combination of both, my name and his name coexisting in the next to the last line:

I never thought you'd go away slowly.

I never thought you'd rush by.
Onto a world I've seen only shadows of.
Here in the mist where I cry.

If you're happy, make the wind blow.
If you're happy, be a star.
Let the world shine if you're happy, Andy – Maxy
so that I know how you are.

The words were mostly clear but I hadn't played a piano in years, and had trouble fingering the melody. I was angry at my lack of ability, struggling over the final bar – when it suddenly came back to me. "Oh my God! Grandpa is dead. And standing outside on the terrace. And I'm in here, trying to play this music!" So I ran back down the hall, through the dining room, and out onto the terrace – but Grandpa was gone!

I was furious with myself. He had come all the way from the land of the dead – and I was inside playing music. But the music came from him. Maybe he wanted me to play it. But what did it all mean? I sat down in the chair again, my head racing. How could this have happened? I sat there in a state of total numbness and complete embodied awe, all woven together.

Soon I heard the heavy metal front door bang and I knew that my family was home. A moment or three later Suzanne came to the open door, stepped out onto the terrace, and said to me these exact words – "You look like you've just seen a ghost." And I said to her – "I did."

Had Grandpa not just been there I might have been afraid to tell her what had happened. She and Dad had seen me suffering after the break up of my relationship and I probably would have been afraid they'd think that I was cracking up. But it had just happened, and it didn't occur to me to edit it.

Suzanne sat down beside me, looking shaken herself. Years before my cousin Joan started calling her mother, my Aunt Rachie, "Mama-tushma" and started calling Grandpa "Grampa-tootie," which caught on with all of us. Suzanne reached out a hand and placed it on my forearm and said, trembling, "We were sitting on the bus coming home and talking about Grampatootie – and we realized that it was exactly a year ago today that he came here to visit us for the very last time."

Later we went inside and I told Dad about his dad coming to visit me, a year to the day after his last visit, which had happened while I was still living in Berkeley. And Dad accepted my experience with Grandpa. Who taught me how to meditate all those years before, and whose visit that day changed my life, flooding me with all sorts of new possibilities.

○

Today is February 17th, 2024, and as I sit typing at my desk, I'm remembering sitting on the terrace with Suzanne, looking out at tall buildings in Manhattan in 1974 – with the tall buildings of downtown Oakland rising up above the top of my laptop and the little open datebook on my desk, just beside my laptop – which tells me that today is exactly fifty years since Grandpa died.

CHAPTER 25

Echoing Voices

IN THE MONTHS AFTER THAT, my father's relationship with Suzanne began to deteriorate. I remember them in their bedroom having big fights. One evening when we were home alone, Dad told me that Suzanne wanted me to move out. I'd been exploring gay life in Manhattan, but the bars and clubs in Greenwich Village were noisy and smoke-filled, with sexy guys who drank and smoked pot, none of which worked for me, and they were sleeping around, which didn't work for me either. But around that time I met a group of lesbians who were exploring their spirituality, which appealed to me, and I decided to move to lesbian headquarters in Park Slope, Brooklyn, around the corner from a man I briefly dated, and where I met several of my most beloved lesbian friends, two of who died in the last four years, Lynne and Ellen, and one of whom, Joan, is still a good friend.

Soon after I moved out, Dad told me he was going to go to LA to try to get work as a screenwriter. I met him at Suzanne's to go with him by cab to the airport. I can see where the three of us were standing, she inside and Dad and I in the hallway outside the open front door, when he said to her, "Don't get a new winter coat. I'll be sending for you and the kids soon."

When we got in a cab on our way to the airport Dad told me that he'd lied to me about Suzanne wanting me to move out. That he wasn't planning to come back and wanted me to move out before he did. Thus I got to live through his leaving home a second time, as an incipient adult, not a child, which was a nightmare, as he never once ever even called her! The schmuck! (Sorry, Dad. I still love you, but really…..!)

Not long after I moved into her place Suzanne asked me if I'd paint the living room, which I did, and then slowly the rest of the apartment.

A neighbor liked my work and asked me to paint hers, which led to more painting gigs, including an entire brownstone. But a year later I was tired of being a house painter. Suzanne continually encouraged me to see myself as a writer, something that none of my other parents did, and around that time I met a man at a gay fundraiser who asked me what I did. I took a deep breath and said, "I'm a writer." He smiled, asked me about my job, and I told him I was a house painter. I remember his words, kind and coming from someone about a decade older than me. "This is New York. Actors work as waiters. Musicians drive cabs. Painters can do anything they want. And writers work in bookstores," in a strong Midwestern accent.

Walking down the street one day not long after, in Brooklyn Heights, I saw a sign in a bookstore window: "Help wanted." I went in, made up a bookstore I'd worked in in California, and told them it had gone out of business. I got a call a few days later that they needed help in their other branch – two blocks and around the corner from my new apartment. So there I was, working in the Community Book Store on Seventh Avenue, which is still there! And it was there that my education continued. For the first time in my life, age twenty-four, I had a regular job, got a real pay-check, with rent and gas, electric and telephone bills to pay. I was living in the real world, and enjoying it. And magic continued to happen. Books would literally fall off shelves for me to read, as they had in Santa Barbara, about Hinduism, reincarnation, Taoism, meditation. And amazing novels and short story collections would fall off shelves or be staring at me as I unpacked cartons of books from the distributor.

One day I opened a carton and a fat hardbound book was staring at me, a collection of poems by May Sarton, whose novel *Mrs. Stevens Hears the Mermaids Singing*, which I discovered on a shelf one day, had already captivated me. Kneeling on the floor beside the carton I started flipping through the book – and my eyes were stopped frozen by the first verse of a poem called "The Great Transparencies."

Shaking, I read through the entire poem, then again, and again, alone in the store, with no customers. Words were dancing in my head, loudly – because this was one of the poems that had been recited to me in my dreams when I was a boy, recited to me over and over again, so that I could recite it from memory, words echoing from decades in the past:

> I have been thinking much of these...
> ... the great transparencies...
> ... they are not ever young.

A few days later I wrote May Sarton, in care of her publisher, and told her the story I just told you. She wrote back and for some time we exchanged letters. I got to meet her once when she gave a reading at Barnard College, in an auditorium filled with several hundred women – and four men.

"The Great Transparencies." I am not young, I am no longer young.

CHAPTER 26

Break-up and Wake-up

I WASN'T LIVING IN BENSONHURST, the part of Brooklyn that my grandparents lived in and my parents grew up in, but Park Slope was still Brooklyn, which for me was The Promised Land. My cousin Michael, his soon-to-be ex-wife Paulette, and their two little boys Gabriel and Gideon were living on the next block, I had a job I loved, a nice circle of friends, and loved living one house in and across the street from Prospect Park, which was my vast urban backyard the way that Lake Merritt is now.

One day I was taking the train to Manhattan, and when I looked up – a very handsome young man was looking up at me. Still awkward in my out gay life I looked away, but then a few days later I was walking to the bookstore for work as he walked past me, noticed me, stopped, and started a conversation. It turned out that he was a grad student at Columbia, lived a few blocks away, and worked part-time in a coffee, tea, and spice shop a few blocks down Seventh Avenue from the book store.

We started spending time together, having sex, and I fell quite deeply in love with him and was fascinated by his life and work. Jewish, he'd lived in India and was studying Sanskrit, and had so much to share with me about Indian culture. But sadly for me, our dance was like the one I'd gone through with my first boyfriend – he saw my monogamous desires as possessive, as heterosexist. "If you really love someone," gay men kept telling me, "you don't own them, you don't own their body." Maybe it was both of my parents' many affairs, Dad, and Mom too, in all of their relationships. Or maybe it was just my own nature. When I tried sleeping around – I felt worse.

We made it through a year, he deeply at work on his master's thesis, me writing stories and working in the bookshop. And then in spring everything fell apart. He was furious with me, I felt abandoned and betrayed by him. One afternoon we were having a fight on the phone and I shouted, "This is the worst thing that has ever happened to me!" To which he shouted back, "No it isn't!" and slammed down the receiver, on a phone with an old-fashion dial, a phone still attached to the wall, as this cranky old man who doesn't use a mobile phone still thinks they should be.

It was a sunny warm afternoon, I was sitting on the edge of my bed, and the jolt of his slamming down the phone threw me backwards onto the bed with my feet still on the floor. As I hung up the phone, inside and all around me – I was watching a vivid full-color movie of something that I had not remembered before.

The movie began in the big old house I remembered, with my other set of parents, the ones I once asked my mother about. In our huge house with a music room and servants and a yard and everyone talking in the language I remembered hearing in my dreams when I was a little boy, a language that at three I'd never heard spoken but at twenty-five knew was German. As I watched that movie I watched my past life unfold, only I call it a movie as if I were simply watching it, but it was in 3D and I wasn't just watching it as if it were a dream – I was in it too! It was awakened memory!

I saw my family, who I'd always remembered, and our home, our servants, as the little five year old boy that I was. I didn't know where it was that we were living, but I saw the coming to power of the Nazis in the background, then the foreground. I reexperienced my father taking me aside to tell me that we were going to have to move, and I saw how we went into hiding with a few boxes and suitcases, moving into an artist's studio in the attic of a building that belonged to friends of my father. The five of us were locked in there, my mother, her father, my father, his mother, and little me. My father had a first wife, I think not Jewish, and I had two older half-sisters who lived with her, but they weren't with us.

Locked away from the world I relived how we lived, ate the often-moldy food we were brought by the family friends who were taking care of us, and I relived my needing to be silent all day in a big room with people working underneath us all day – which wasn't easy for a little boy. All five of us slept on the floor of a big room whose huge windows were all painted black, except for a tiny little hole my grandfather scraped off, so that we could look out. I had seen fireworks before the war and one day I looked out onto what me-the-watcher knew was a bombing, but which the little me in the attic did not understand and thought were fireworks. And I turned six up in the attic, a little boy whose name I learned was Josef, who was given a little party and a little sweet treat to eat.

One day not long after that we were all sitting on the floor when there was the sound of loud footsteps thundering up the stairs, and someone banged on the door and then smashed it open. I was terrified – then excited. My mother's father had fought in the First World War, was very proud of his service, and there were pictures of him in uniform around the house. So I was terrified of the door being smashed open, then excited by the men in uniform, terrified again as I saw and heard what they wanted us to do and felt the terror my family was experiencing.

We were taken away to a large sealed room, then taken somewhere else, and then crammed in a train for days. I remember desperately needing to pee, but don't remember what I did, and I remember looking up and out the tiny slit of a window that ran along the length of the car, up by the ceiling. And I remember how a girl around twelve years old died standing up beside me, but we were so packed in that there was nowhere to move or lay down her body. Then the train pulled to a stop and we were all ordered out. It was a gorgeous day, with a perfect blue sky.

There were parallel rows of tracks and low buildings all around us. I heard a man in uniform yell at all the men and older boys to go off to one side, and the women and little kids to stay where we were. My father and grandfather went off to the left with all the other men, and then the officer told all of us that we had to take off our clothes. I had on two coats, one on top of the other, and my sleeve got stuck as I tried to get out of them. Seeing that, my mother slapped me and my father's mother turned to her with rage in her eyes that I somehow knew meant something like, "You stupid bitch. We're all about to die – and you go and slap your little boy?!"

Die. Some deeper wisdom rose up in me and I knew and understood what that meant, from other past lives. Then we were crammed into a room, a room full of naked women of all ages and naked little girls and boys. I was six, from a very proper German-Jewish family, and I had never seen anyone naked before. Ever. Fascinated and repelled, as the room filled with gas we all began coughing and choking, some people louder than others, some screaming and shouting. Horrified by what was happening and by seeing my very proper mom and my Oma, Grandma, naked, gasping for breath, I looked around, brokenhearted.

Then there was a moment when I felt a contraction in my chest, and I can only describe it this way – my soul rose up out of the top of my head, rose up a foot or two and then was pulled back into my body. Then it happened another time, only my soul rose up a little higher, all the way up to the ceiling of the gas chamber. Then it happened a third time, and my soul rose up through the ceiling and out into the glorious day that was happening all around us, only to be pulled all the way back down into my body. Then it happened again – my soul rose up out of my body, up and out the top of my head, up and out of the gas chamber, up and out and through the gorgeous sky, and I felt a kind of shudder and snap of disconnection in the middle of my chest – and I was:

a – free

b – released

c – dead.

I felt like myself, Josef, the little boy who I was. I was his/my own shape and size, but I knew that I was only my soul, and I found myself somehow standing in a place that I can only to this day describe as being a field of infinite blueness, a different blue than the sky I'd left behind, a bit more cobalt. An infinite field of luminous blue that I was somehow standing in, but which had no gravity, no top or bottom – although that doesn't make sense to me as I type, but did make sense as I was remembering it, being in it.

Then in the distance I saw a light, a growing light, as something, as someone came toward me. It, she, was a tall luminous woman who my Andrew brain translated as what Josef identified as "The Grandmother." I think that he was thinking that she was his mother's mother, who had died before he was born. She was smiling, lovely, warm, and when she asked him very gently if he knew that he was dead he told her that he did. Then she asked him if there was anywhere that he wanted to go, and he, and I, said "Yes, I want to go home again, one more time."

The next thing I knew – we were back in the front room of our big old house. Both my parents were musicians. Mom played the violin and Dad played the piano. One of my favorite things to do was to lie underneath that big grand piano when he was rehearsing. And we had lots of recitals there, which I loved too. I wandered around the room – was it the actual room or a hologram? To this day I don't know. But it looked and felt like that room, and being there gave me a deep sense of joy and completion. After a while The Grandmother asked me if I was ready to go on, and I said yes.

She took my hand and led me to the closed sliding double doors that led to the front entryway, to the stairs and the front door. She stopped and said not to be afraid, as the paneled doors slid open on their own. On the other side there was a solid wall of what I can only describe as – fire. She said again to not be afraid, and holding my hand she led me into the fire. To my amazement it was ice cold, not hot, and after walking through it for about ten feet we came to the other side and found ourselves in a glorious tree-filled garden, only – and to this day I have trouble understanding or explaining it – everything I was looking at in the garden was gold – all of it gold – only the gold of a tall tree's leaves was as different from the gold of its bark as green leaves are different from a tree's brown bark. Across from us, sitting on a stone bench, was a very old bearded man, and standing all around him were hundreds of other people, all of them somehow familiar, although I had no idea who they were.

The Grandmother led me up to the old man, who welcomed me and told me, "You know where you are. And you know that you don't have to go back." I may have only been six but I looked up at him and said, in what language or in pure telepathy I cannot say – "Look at what's going on down there. How can I not go back?!"

I felt then as if there were a gigantic computer whirling all around me, searching through all of my past lives, exploring all of my karmic connections to people who were alive on the earth. Souls, people, places, were flashing all around me, and then everything stopped and I knew that three different couples had been chosen to be my future parents. One by one I met them, saw them, felt them, learned about them. A very comfortable London family with a big old house and lots of wonderful connections. An amazingly rich Dutch Malay couple who lived on a vast plantation in Indonesia. And then a not-rich couple living in New York. I saw the mom-to-be, but what captivated me was the dad. He was sitting on a stoop in uniform, somewhere in Europe. I was looking down at him and said to myself, "He's so full of dreams." I knew that he was the one I wanted to be my next daddy, and told that to the old man on the bench.

As soon as I let him know – the double in spirit, if I may call it that, of my little Josef body began to melt down and expand into a shining sphere of light about eight feet in diameter. I was that sphere, I was me, somehow, and I turned around and saw that above and behind me what looked like the large iris of an eye was opening, opening wide enough for me to pass through it. And I did.

Time? I'm not sure. Space? Across the universe. All at once I – that luminous sphere – was passing through the wall of a building and surrounding a double bed in which a woman and a man were making passionate love. The woman was my mommy in this life and the man was my daddy, who I'd already met while in uniform. They were making love – inside of me! Inside of the vast luminous sphere of me! And I could see the room, their double bed pushed into the corner by a window. I could see a familiar brown corduroy headboard that I, Andy, recognized from the bed that Mommy and Daddy slept in behind the bookcase in our apartment in Elmhurst, which came with us to their bedroom in Rockville Centre. I knew that Grandma had covered the headboard and made a matching bedspread for that bed, and I knew, as the huge sphere of me slowly merged with Gerry and Jack's bodies, that they were making love in the studio apartment they lived in before I was born, in the same building we all lived in, upstairs, that they moved to when Mommy was pregnant with me.

As Mommy started to orgasm, I began to shrink down so that I could enter her body, and as I did so – I began to come back to being just me, Andrew, lying on my back with my feet on the floor, on my bed in my bedroom on the third floor of 863 Carroll Street in Brooklyn.

To this day I can only tell you that I think that whole experience lasted for about twenty minutes of in-the-world clock time. And then – I was back. Me. Andrew Ramer.

I sat up, amazed, in awe, grateful in a way to my ex-boyfriend for screaming at me and initiating that amazing experience, unlike anything that had ever happened to me before, and unlike anything I'd ever read about.

I sat up and looked around, around at my lovely familiar room. And my bed, my books, fireplace, mantelpiece, my prize possessions sitting on top of it, and then down at the lovely parquet wood floor. Light was pouring through the two windows, and for the first time in my life all the parts of me felt like they had come together – my earliest Andy memories, my other parents, my existence as a soul. And for the first time in my life I knew that I wasn't crazy, a mistake, psychotic. I knew in every light-filled cell in my body that I had just had a spiritual mystical transformative experience. I knew that The Grandmother was how my guardian angel Sargolais had come to and revealed it/her/himself to Josef. And all of that changed me in a deep way that I am so grateful for.

○

I sat on my bed for about twenty minutes, in awe, unable to move. Then I picked up the phone and called my ex to thank him for initiating what happened, but didn't tell him what it was. Then I called my mother, got her at home, and told her. She knew I'd been on a kind of spiritual journey so what I related wasn't utterly strange to her. When I asked her about their bed and the headboard cover that Grandma had made for it, and if they already had it in that studio apartment, Mom said yes, but when I came to the end of the story and described how the bed was pushed all the way in the corner she said no, that I was wrong – and a bit of doubt began to flicker in me, not enough to doubt everything, but my usual doubt – was that all just my imagination?

The experience did allow me to make an odd connection in my mind. From as far back as I could remember, and to that very day – food that had gone bad – horrified, terrified me! Lettuce turning black around the edges in the bottom of the refrigerator? I had to throw it out! An old pot of soup that I wanted to reheat for dinner? When I took off the lid and saw mold growing on it, I had to throw it out. An apple, a banana, turning brown? In the garbage! (We didn't have composting yet!) And for the first time I understood that out-of-proportion horror, remembering what my family and I had to eat, up in that attic. Dad only played jazz and Broadway show tunes. And I remembered the day after he left when Mom came home with a boxed set of records of all of Beethoven's symphonies. It was love at first sound, and when Mommy and Richie weren't home I would blast them on the phonograph and dance in ecstasy around the living room. And all at once – remembering my childhood as Josef and what went on in our music room – I understood why! Those were the other parents I had asked my mother about.

A few days later I was at home when the phone rang. When I picked it up it was Mom, sounding frantic. She asked me to describe the room again and when I did she said, "When we knew that we were ready to start a family, your father and I put in for a larger apartment. One day we were out in the world and he found a desk that he really liked, but when we brought it back to the apartment – it was too small to fit anywhere – so we slid our bed down the wall into the corner – just the way that you described it. But we lived there for four years and moved soon after he got the desk, up to the apartment that you remember – and I forgot all about our bed being in the corner!"

A few days after my experience, and after my first conversation with my mother, I called up Merl, my stepfather. He'd been a Nazi prisoner of war, and I called to ask him about the box car. When I described it and mentioned the long narrow slit of a window I remembered looking up at, he told me that he'd been in box cars and that I was wrong.

A few days later I was at home again when the phone rang. It was Merl, who only called me one other time – ever! He asked me to tell him how old I was in the story that I'd told him, which wasn't so far out of his field of perception. He could always tell when someone was going to die, about two weeks before they did. He said he could see their aura disappearing, even if they weren't sick but died in a car accident. When I told him I was six he said, "You're right. There *were* narrow windows in those box cars. But they were at eye-level for an adult – and if you were six you would have had to look up at them, just as you said!"

Some time not long after that I read *Black Elk Speaks* by John Neihardt, an American poet and writer. It's the story of Black Elk, an Oglala Lakota medicine man. When I came upon the line that warriors would say on their way off to battle, "Today is a good day to die," I thought back to the glorious day when I stepped out of that train, and I understood.

It's odd that other than a few short trips across the border to Canada and Mexico, the only foreign countries I've ever spent time in were Israel for my junior year and then three weeks in – of all places – Germany – where I taught two week-long residential retreats for gay men in two different places, with a week in between with Randy my lover in a pension in the Black Forest. We also stayed for a few days in Hamburg, and wandering around the city, parts of it looked and felt familiar, and I wondered if that was where Josef and his family lived. (Randy is a wonderful writer. Look him up. Randy Lee Higgins.)

○

One afternoon a few years later I was sitting on the subway, on the Upper West Side of Manhattan, not far from where I'd first seen David. I was reading; no recollection of what. But I do remember that I looked up as the train was pulling into the next station, and noticed an older man seated across from me, slightly to my left. He was white, wearing a brownish winter coat and a brown fedora, and looked to be in his seventies. For a moment I stared at him, puzzled by how familiar he looked, although I knew that I'd never seen him before. And then – as he slowly moved to stand up and leave the train – I started crying! I watched his back as he left the car, walked down the platform, as the train pulled out, amazed, as nothing like that had ever happened to me before, or has since – those spontaneous tears. I cried for a minute or two, then stopped, utterly puzzled. And it was only a few hours later, when I was back in my apartment, that all of a sudden it occurred to me – "Oh my God! That was my father, Josef's father! He didn't die! He survived!!" Awe, grief, amazement, wonder poured through me. For weeks I took the same train, hoping to see him again. Imagining how I might go up to him and say.... what? But I never once saw him again, and had the sense a few months later that he had died.

PART 3

Growing and Grown

CHAPTER 27

A Contact Memory

MOM'S ATHEIST FAMILY SHAPED her life for years. We always had a Seder, lit Hanukkah candles, she went with us to High Holiday services until Dad left, and kept Richie and me in Hebrew School after he was gone and through our bar mitzvahs, but there was no other Jewish ritual life in our home and Mom was a big fan of bacon and Chinese food, all non-kosher. When Rich and I were in college she decided to go to college herself, went on to grad school and became what was then called a Marriage, Family, and Child Counselor. One of her grad school professors was Navaho, and she opened Mom up to spirituality for the first time, which made it much easier for me to talk with her about what was going on in my life.

One spring Mom came to visit me in my little two-room apartment in Brooklyn. I gave her my bed and slept in a sleeping bag on the floor in the other room. The second afternoon that she was there we were sitting at my kitchen table, talking. I'd put up a kettle of water to make a pot of tea and took out two lovely Japanese raku teacups that I bought the previous weekend at an outdoor art fair in Manhattan. When I was little, Mom had taken a pottery class and had loved Japanese art since she was a little girl, and again, her mother had read her stories from *Little Pictures of Japan*, which she would later read to me. So Mom was admiring the cups as the tea steeped, and we were chatting about nothing in particular, just catching up.

When I filled the first cup and handed it to her – something shifted in the room. I had my left hand on one side of the cup, Mom was holding the other side with her right, our fingers touching, and she looked at me and said, "Something is happening." I could feel it too and said so. "The room is vanishing," Mom said, and I could see that too. All at once the two of us were someplace else. We were sitting on the floor across from each other – in what was a very small and simple Japanese room. We could both see it and described it to each other. And then Mom said, just as I was about to, "But I'm not me anymore. I'm an old man. A pottery master. And you are a young man, and one of my students!"

In that other place we were sitting on the floor, conscious of both our present selves and our past selves, and it was very clear what was happening. Mom gave it words. "I'm your teacher, and you just handed me a cup that you'd made, and I looked it over, turned it around, and said to you that it was very good."

Then I added. "Yes. For the very first time when I handed you a cup you said it was good, that it was good enough for the first time to glaze and fire."

We sat there holding the cup, that didn't look anything like the cup the other two of us were holding in our shared past. And we sat there looking at each other in a state of utter amazement, as the room slowly turned back into my little Park Slope kitchen, Mom and I turned back into Gerry and Andrew. Then I filled up the second raku cup, and we sipped our tea, and talked through, over and over again, what had just happened to us, which we'd bring up over the years until she died, in 1999. Another past life in Japan, which explained to me why after my year of living in Jerusalem I promised myself that I would one day live in Kyoto for a year. So far, not.

○

This happened to me two more times in my life, once in the early 80s with my late dear friend Barbara Shor, who died in 2000, who I will tell you more about later – when we remembered having been siblings in Italy during the Renaissance, a long-necked sister and brother who everyone called "the swans." Some years later I was sitting with a boyfriend in Dolores Park in San Francisco and at the same moment each of us said to the other, "You're wearing a turban!" and we found ourselves back in a shared past life years before when we were gay lovers, one older than the other, one of whom was killed in battle, leaving the other one in despair. And over the years, not with such clarity, and with increasing frequency since I've moved to Oakland, I'll meet someone and we'll feel such a deep connection that one or the other or both of us at the same time will say – "Wow! I think we knew each other in a past life."

For years I've remembered having been born on the East Coast as a Native American gay man, two thousand five hundred years ago, long before the Europeans invaded, in the region I've spent so much time in this life in North Carolina, where the Gay Spirit Visions Conference is held. In that life my partner (whose name translates into English as Blue Hand) and I studied with a wise gay elder named Crow Medicine, and then we wandered the Americas teaching what he taught us to others, and ended up living here in Oakland. My name in that life was Talking Deer, and many years ago I took dictation from Blue Hand that can be found in an unpublished book *Five Wisdom Teachers*.

CHAPTER 28

My First Blessing

THE EXACT YEAR I CAN'T RECALL, 1977 or 1978, perhaps. I'm living in Brooklyn, still working in the Community Bookstore and going from one boyfriend to another, but mainly socializing with women, most of them lesbians, many of them writers and artists. A few have remained my friends down through the years, as I've mentioned, but sadly two of them, Ellen Melamed and Lynne Reynolds, both died in the last three years.

I remember several evenings sitting around in my then-and still-friend Joan Larkin's home. I was one of two men, both of us gay, who she would sometimes invite to parties. I don't remember his name, but he died of AIDS a long time ago. And I don't remember what led up to it that evening, nor did Joan – who was and is a wonderful poet – check out her work! – when I asked her about it a year or two ago. And we weren't sure if poet Adrienne Rich was there that evening. We remembered other evenings when she was, and one when she was sitting in a large orange-velvet-covered armchair, talking about writing, when I was literally sitting at her feet, learning from her. So perhaps she was there that night, or not, but Joan and I both remember that those two amazing poets Audre Lorde and June Jordan were there, as they often were when I was there, June alone and Audre with her partner Frances and sometime with their two kids.

Almost everyone was standing around in Joan's large kitchen. There was a carved wooden spoon hanging up on the wall, the handle about four feet long, the bowl about six inches wide and eight inches long.. Joan took it off the wall and asked me to kneel on the linoleum floor in front of her, with everyone else surrounding us. And then, like the queen in a movie from a long time ago, Joan tapped my left shoulder with her long wooden spoon, then my right shoulder, and said, looking down at me: "I hereby dub thee an honorary lesbian."

My cells were tingling and filled with light, and I felt whole in a way that I had not felt in years. Felt that all of my binary past lives, female and male, were fully united in my one living breathing body. Today we live with they/them pronouns and more and more of us identify as non-binary, but that wasn't the case then. There wasn't what we call today a queer community. We were lesbians and gay men. And kneeling on the floor, looking up at Joan, her kitchen counter right behind her, in a room filled with lesbian artists and performers and teachers and painters and poets – I felt blessed and whole and holy and slowly got up to my feet smiling, as everyone in the kitchen began to applaud.

CHAPTER 29

The Door Opens Wide

MY SOCIAL STUDIES BOOK awakened me to ancient Egypt, which I was fascinated with for quite some time, and then somebody gave me a picture book of Greek myths for my birthday, which opened a whole other door to my next great love. I took every book out of the library that I could find on the subject, feeling for the first time that I had a model for reality that made sense to me. Not one God but many, a whole new idea to me, gods and goddess in story after story after story. A total delight! And down through the years I continued to read and reread those Greek myths, finding something there that I couldn't/didn't find anywhere else.

Erick came into my life and changed it, changed me, opened me up to Hindu myths and stories that I hadn't known about before, that echoed into deep inward places as ancient Egypt and ancient Greece had. Awakening soft whispers inside me from my past. You know the story about hearing God talk to me in Jerusalem, and how Rabbi Fox turned off my voices. In fact, I forgot all about them, graduated from Berkeley, moved back to New York, and was working in that bookstore in Park Slope, Brooklyn, with an occasional boyfriend and my circle of lesbian friends – certainly not what the rabbi would ever have imagined, but my version of just what he had ordered.

In 1976, a voice started speaking to me one morning while I was in the shower. My first voice in around five years. He spoke with an odd English accent and claimed to have introduced William Shakespeare to his mysterious male lover. Each morning he'd be there as I stood beneath the water, reciting endless verses of Elizabethan poetry that may have been his own and that I thought were terrible. For the first time however, I wasn't afraid

– I was annoyed! – and told him to go away, which he did. But before he left he warned me that my next 'visitor' would be harder to get rid of.

A few weeks later, on the night of the spring equinox in 1977 I was eating dinner in Minsky's, a restaurant down the street from the bookstore where I worked. One of the waitresses, Linda Sherwood, was an actress who frequently came into the store to buy another copy of a book on channeling called *Seth Speaks,* by Jane Roberts. I had only read the back cover, never once connected it to my own experiences, and frankly thought that it was ridiculous. So while I quite liked Linda, I questioned her sanity, just as our culture had taught me to do. Still, our friendship grew and deepened, over tables and counters, living in the same neighborhood and even on the same block, we soon discovered.

Linda was tired on that equinox night, of having to waitress in order to act, of not being able to get acting work, and was thinking about quitting the theatre. As she moved from table to table, stopping to talk when she had a chance, I unfolded my paper napkin and began to write down all sorts of reasons why she shouldn't give up acting. "The theatre is holy," I wrote. "The actor is the opposite of a priest." I read the words over, feeling scared, because those were not my thoughts, not my words. I soon developed a splitting headache, gave Linda the napkin, paid my bill, and ran home.

Out of breath, I sat down at my kitchen table, in the seat my mother had been sitting in when we opened up to the past, feeling as if someone were trying to force a broomstick up through the top of my head. Wondering if I were finally going crazy, feeling that everything in my life was changing too fast to make sense of, I thought back to Rabbi Fox's words, realized I had a solid job and good connections with my family and friends, and knew that if I did crack up I'd be well taken care of. So I grabbed a pen and pad, an instant reflex after seven years of keeping a journal. If I was going crazy, I wanted to keep a record of it.

Everything became dark. Not outside, but within me. I was staring into an endless dark vault – from an eye perched inside my head, at the top of my spine. "Is this insanity?" I asked myself. I wasn't afraid of it. Didn't fight it. Suddenly I felt as if I were sliding halfway out of my body to the left, and felt as if someone else was sliding halfway into me from the right. Was I being possessed? I feared as much. But where we touched, in the center of my body, and where we met in the center of the darkness in my head – a light flashed. I could see it with a third inner eye. I watched the light converge into several glowing, humming, colored, geometric shapes:

a cube, a sphere, a pyramid, each one fully visible from all sides at once, each one fully visible – even though they all occupied the same space. And the shapes had meaning! Was that madness? I picked up my pen and wrote down what I knew the shapes meant: "Aeschylus Notes".

Everything went dark again. "If this is madness, it isn't so terrible," I thought. "I have good friends and family who will take care of me. I might as well keep going." Then a second shape flashed, a more complex one, with cones and rods and changing colors. This shape also had meaning. Somehow I understood what it meant, and wrote down: "The words of a student of Aeschylus, from remembered pieces of class work".

Aeschylus, the Greek playwright, who looked so dry to me in college that I read Sophocles instead? A student of Aeschylus? I felt him in my body. Was I possessed? Perhaps. But his presence felt not just benign but benevolent. And while I knew at that moment that I could throw him out if I wanted to – I let him remain, wanted him to remain, wanted to find out why he was there and what was happening to me. And having made that decision – I crossed fully over the threshold between times and worlds.

A third shape flashed, larger and more intricate. When I tried to look at it directly it faded, but when I looked away the shape opened, not just into words or into meaning; it opened into vision as well. I was looking through someone's eyes, out across an empty stone stage, up, into a brilliant, cloudless sky. And then a man began to speak, an older bearded man who was standing up on that outdoor stone stage. His words flashed across time and into those geometric shapes, all his words coming to me in a thought-knot, all his words coming at the same time. But somehow, I knew what they all meant, and began to write them down.

For over an hour I worked with the shapes, bringing the words out, watching Aeschylus talk. Watching the other students, all of us young men. Filling up ten pages of quickly scrawled words, until the last shape faded into darkness, until the visiting presence slipped out, and the darkness was replaced by the return of my little white kitchen.

I felt selfless and pure as I wrote, but when I started to read over what I had written, I wondered again if I had gone crazy, because half of what was there did not make sense to me. I'd never read Aeschylus, never acted, although I'd lived on the edge of my father writing plays and Suzanne acting in and directing them, but as I read what came through me, sentence followed sentence, with a logic quite beyond me. Or no logic, only madness. Terrified of what had just happened, I grabbed my coat and ran back to the restaurant, knowing that Linda would still be there. I burst in, interrupted her in the middle of a conversation, said, "I just wrote this. Please read it and call me in the morning."

The sun woke me. I stretched and heard myself say, "There's no going back now." I felt as if I'd been married – or murdered. That I would never be the same again. Joy and terror swept through me, as I thought of the pages I'd given to Linda, as I thought about the nature of thought itself, of writing, of the way that we begin a sentence trusting that somehow meaning will unfold, each linear sentence carrying us on to the next unplanned sentence. So I had written ten pages without thinking at all. I had emptied myself out completely, in order to write down someone else's thoughts, or thoughts from a place in myself that I had no access to at other times. Forgetting about the shapes that I'd seen, the words that I'd put down on paper had flown through me and onto paper effortlessly, without the terrible struggle that writing a poem or a story always entailed for me, where experience and imagination have to be welded into coherent meaning. Had I gone mad? I looked around me. The bed, walls, books, and mantle in my room looked more solid than ever, more real, as if I'd stepped, not out of the world but more fully into it. And then the phone rang, clearly and loudly.

It was Linda, calling to tell me how true and how real the words were, to ask how I wrote them. "So I'm not going crazy," I told myself. "It makes sense. Beneath the words there is real life experience, real thought. It isn't just ten pages of nonsense. Linda says so. She acts. She ought to know." So I told her everything that had happened to me the evening before.

That night I sat down at the kitchen table again, sensing there were still more words inside me, wondering if I could connect with them myself or if I had to wait for them to reach me. But having had that amazing opening happen to me once, it was easier to make my mind empty again, to feel someone beside me, then slipping inside me. And as soon as he did, I could see the shapes flash again.

A few nights a week I would do it, empty out and write, then give the pages to Linda, waiting for her to call each time and reassure me – that I wasn't going crazy, that the book inspired her. The more I read the words I was transcribing, the more I began to understand, or to remember. I slowly came to feel that I was in touch with a past aspect of myself, intimate and familiar, that I had been the student of Aeschylus, the real author of the book, who had been waiting for centuries to find a way to tell his story.

○

As remarkable as it was to have stumbled into my past, the nature of the flashes was even more remarkable. It seemed that purely by accident I had become a witness to the very workings of telepathy. On the subway, when I listened to people talking, I could almost see the flashing of shapes from head to head. I kept wanting to go up to people and say, "You think you understand each other because you're both talking English. But you really understand each other because geometric shapes are flashing between you, which convey the essence of speech back and forth." Even foreign languages (and animal languages) seemed within my ability to understand, if only I could grasp the shapes. But if I tried to watch them flashing they faded, and eventually even the book stopped, when my inner visitor had said all that he had to say, and I was left with those handwritten pages and the waking dream of a visual, universal language, of a geometric-light-shape dictionary, based on the deep inner hieroglyphics of all human communication.

Was I really looking into ancient Greece? Had I reached my own past, the collective unconscious, or a new deep level of my own imagination? I felt when the experience was first happening that if it wasn't really ancient Greece, the book was worthless. But over the years I've come to feel that the value of that book isn't its historicity but its being the chronicle of a profoundly moving experience, unlike anything that ever happened to me before, that happens to few of us, and still fills me with awe at our untapped potential.

There were snags in the process. Sometimes a shape flashed for something I did not know. "Word-making stick." Was it a pen, a quill, a stylus? Or "frothy drink." Was it beer? Then I saw what I knew was a slang word for money. I wrote "coppers," but were they? I couldn't tell. Maybe they were silver, or tin. And when personal names flashed, where sound and not just meaning had to be conveyed, the whole process stopped. To this day I'm not sure about Chrysos and Periclides, which I first spelled as Chrysus and Paraclides, only to later look up and discover that they were real Greek names. But each time Aeschylus spoke someone's name I felt I was struggling through time itself to grasp the sound that fell from his lips, perhaps the way that people who sign spell out a letter at a time the names of people and places.

During those nights when I was sitting at my kitchen table, I felt that I was watching a strange movie unfold from the center of my brain in a full wrap-around projection, not just of sight and sound but with feeling, temperature, even smells. I was observing an older bearded man. A moody man. A man of joy and sorrow, who could retreat into silence one moment, and then reach out to tease one of his students, a flirt, a haughty youth, a tease himself. He pulled their daily lives into his lectures. I could see their world as he spoke. The theatres, the markets, his garden. I was looking through the mind of his student. Through a window, not glass-filled, but open to the wind. There were days when I was so alive in the past that not just the particulars of the dictation but line after line of lost, forgotten Greek plays washed through me, just beyond my conscious ability to capture them.

For thirty-nine nights I took dictation. When the writing was done I gave the pages to a friend, Sue Renee Bernstein, who typed them up for me. Alas, the original pages vanished long ago, as did the napkin I gave to Linda on the night my adventure began – it disappeared once when she was moving.

The account of the unfolding adventure in my journal is sketchy at best, failing to supply many of the details I would include if it happened to me now. But my story remains, and the story of the book remains, and somewhere along the way my memory opened up more fully, and I realized that although one of my fellow students, Chrysos, was flirty and hot and sexy, that I was the young man Aeschylus courted and took to his bed. And I remembered a time when Aeschylus sat me down and talked about Chrysos, who had just given a truly marvelous performance, and told me that I wasn't fated to be an actor – but a writer, just like he was himself! I remembered being in his bed, making love, in his garden, at his table sharing a meal. And as my memories rose to the surface I watched myself grow ill as Periclides, watched that wise wonderful brilliant older man take care of me, and then I watched myself die in his bed, in his arms. And I could feel Periclides' unfulfilled creativity rising up in me, in this me, who two thousand and five hundred years later is doing my best to fulfill his potential in another body – something that you my be doing too!

CHAPTER 30

And Light Pours In

AFTER I FINISHED TAKING dictation from Periclides, a past self, I stepped back into my ordinary life, feeling enriched, expanded, and renewed. Not long after, on the afternoon of Saturday May 7th 1977 I was sitting on my bed about to put my shoes on – when the room began to change. Everything solid seemed to be made out of something like clouds – the walls, the bed, and even myself. I felt a powerful gathering of silence swirling around me, and then the entire universe somehow became visible – as a vast enormous disc resting on the top of my head. Next, from the outermost edges of that huge disc – a circular wave of golden light began to wash in toward the center, where it poured into an opening on the top of my head. The waves were light and the light was a voice, a voice of this and every other world.

Hello, the voice said, in one and yet in a million different languages, a warm female voice that poured into the top of my head, in wave after golden wave of liquid light. Awed, split open, filled with bliss, I felt as if my life was just beginning, not at my birth but in that middle moment. Then the voice and the wave receded, and I turned to the being who had just spoken, and said, "Who are you?" Again, from the outermost edge of the disc another circular wave came toward me, pouring into the top of my head. "You know who I am," the warm female voice said. Then the waves retreated, but I still didn't understand and repeated, "Who are you?" Again, the same answer came in an in-rushing thunder of gold. "You know who I am," and the truth awakened inside me, but not yet believing, I asked a third time, "Who are you?" And the voice that came washing into me, in wave upon golden wave, was louder than it had been before. "You know who I am,"

Then there was silence, a retreat of waves, and an advance again of light-words, this time more thunderous then anything that had come before, or since, and She said to me –

You know who I am!
I am the Great Mother.
I am that from which all things come.

Then the thunder of Her voice retreated to the outer edge of that infinite golden disc, a voice that I could hear by seeing, and see with sound. A voice that was also a million voices at the same time, and yet always a warm, strong, gentle, caring female voice, who answered my next question, "Why have you come?" in a tone both challenging and teasing – "To torment you!" – which made me laugh.

"What should I call You?" I asked Her next. "Call me anything you like. Call me Mother, or God. Call Me Aphrodite." I knew by Aphrodite that She didn't mean the goddess of love, the daughter of Zeus, but a goddess far more ancient: Aphrodite the Queen of Heaven, a manifestation of the way that our earliest ancestors first encountered the Divine, as God the Mother. Being a long-time lover of Greek mythology, that was the name I chose. Next I asked Her how I should worship Her, and She filled my head with laughing images of fiery altars of sacrifice and long lines of priests, and said that the only thing She wanted from me was that I write a book. My immediate response was, "There are too many books in the world already, and I don't want to add to that mess." She had no comment, so I asked, "But why me?" In fact I asked that question many times in the days and weeks to come, and She always answered – "Why *not* you?" To which I said, "But I'm not a lesbian, or even a woman." She laughed when I said that and answered, "I talk to who I want to."

○

So began an amazing year in my life, in which Her voice, which I heard at first on the outside of my head, began to settle down into a glowing spot in the very center of my brain, a place where I'd never heard a voice before. And instead of speaking in an infinite number of languages, Her voice settled down into English, my mother tongue. In order to hear Her, all that I had to do was to bring my attention to that spot. And I surrendered to Her request – sitting at my kitchen table to take dictation.

For several days during that time I entered a state of awareness in which I knew that *everything* was Her. I remember sitting on the toilet one morning in tears, knowing She was the toilet seat, my butt, poop, the toilet paper I was pulling off the roll. I managed to rein in that awareness to go out into the world, but later, walking home on Flatbush Avenue, I came upon a homeless man passed out on the sidewalk in a puddle of urine. I stepped into the street to get by him, over cigarette butts and pop-tops from beer cans – and I knew in every fiber of my being that the drunken man, the sidewalk, his urine flowing down into the street, the tossed cigarette butts and those discarded pop-tops – were all Her. Weeping, staggering in the street, I said to Her, "This is too much for me to handle. I'll never be able to get home if I keep feeling this. Please take it away." In that instant I returned to my usual state of consciousness, and I've never again had an experience quite like that – yet it's permeated every moment since of living in Her world. I often hear love songs as prayers, and these experiences echo in and out of one that you may know, which was first recorded in 1971 by a soul group called The Stylistics – "You are everything, and everything is You."

She began dictating to me as Aphrodite, but soon began to change, so slowly that I could never say quite when the wise, warm, older Aphrodite had changed into a younger, more intimate Inanna, the ancient Sumerian goddess. Then She shifted again, so gradually that I couldn't tell when chummy chatty Inanna became the tranquil, compassionate Buddhist goddess of mercy, Quan Yin, speaking to me in the same voice, in the same place in my brain, with a slightly different "accent." She dictated Book One of Her teachings to me a word at a time, gave me the words to Book Two a paragraph at a time, then for Book Three She dropped thoughts into my mind that I had to shift around, playing with words until She said, "That's right. Keep it."

While I was working on Book Three She began to shift again, like water, constantly changing. I knew Her as Earth one day, Moon the next, then as the Wiccan Maid-Mother-Crone Triple Goddess, and then She came to me as Sarada Devi, the wife of the 19th century Indian mystic Ramakrishna. In the midst of an at-home retreat, for the very first time since She'd come to me – She was vast, silent, allowing me to encounter Her as The Void. This, She told me, is easier to open up to when we know God as She, the Void an absence with Him and a vast Openness, pregnant with possibility, when we know God as Goddess. Then She appeared in my bedroom one morning as the ancient Egyptian goddess Isis, standing beside me, solidly present, extending a hand to me and touching me, physically, which never happened again, placing an energetic ankh, the ancient Egyptian symbol of life, in the middle of my right hand. After that She began to show Herself to me as an elegant grey-haired Jewish-looking woman in her mid-sixties, whose name, She told me, was Lia. I could see Her when I sat quietly and turned inward, and it was in that period that She gave me Book Four. I would write down the words that came to me, shift and rearrange them, add to them, and wait for Her to whisper, "Yes."

○

I never sought out the voice of God, nor was I drinking or smoking pot or taking hallucinogenic substances. I didn't think I believed in God at all when first She came to me, and was initially stunned that God might be She and not He. And the questions that interest me now aren't, "Why does God speak to me?" but: "What circumstances made it such that I could listen?" And – "Why aren't you listening too?" My best answers – remembering my death in a Nazi gas chamber and being raised in this life with just the right combination of faith and doubt, has shaped me in such a way that I'm able to hear voices that others usually do not, or cannot, the same way that a dog can hear a dog whistle. Not crazy. Just canine. Can't drive. Can't dribble a basketball. But I've been told again and again by Her, by guides and angels, that skills like this are inherited biological traits that some of us have strongly, others not so strongly, and that's why some of us can hear things that most other people can't – consciously! Because, I've been told over and over again, down through the years, that She and the angels and our ancestors and guides and the Earth itself are speaking to us all the time – unconsciously.

She's been speaking to me ever since, in varying ways that you'll hear more about. I continue to take dictation from Her, and sitting in Her energy field is part of my meditation practice, which I try to do twice a day – with occasional success. So dear reader, please consider that you too might be a prophet. And that even if you're not – She's whispering to you, to us, all the time.

CHAPTER 31

My Next Visitation

IN 1978 MY FATHER was diagnosed with a brain tumor. I flew out to LA to be with him after his surgery, and to see other family. I was visiting cousins for a weekend and woke up one morning to find that the right side of my face was totally numb. Scared, when I got to my mother's a day later, I went to see her doctor who diagnosed me as having something that I'd never heard of before – Bell's Palsy. I liked the name but was frightened when I looked in the mirror and saw the right side of my face drooped down and frozen.

Mom had resisted my love of Egypt. Egypt for her, even ancient Egypt, was our enemy as Jews, down through time – but she totally supported my love of ancient Greece and Greek mythology and continued to buy me books on the subject, some of which I still have. Well, not still have. They went off in a box to the Pacific School of Religion, where my papers are archived, but I feel like I still have them.

When I was around fourteen Mom brought me a wonderful plaque of the ancient Greek god of healing, Aesculapius. The plaque is made of fired clay that's the green of tarnished brass, and on it is a handsome man perhaps in his thirties, bearded, wearing a toga, with his left shoulder exposed. (As I write this now I realize for the very first time – and it's 2024 now – that his exposed left shoulder is the same as mine was when I discovered my mole more than seventy years ago!) Aesculapius is standing beside the vertical carving of his name in ancient Greek letters, his right hand on a staff with a snake coming up it. The snake appears with other ancient goddesses and gods, and we know it in this country as a symbol for doctors and for medicine.

Mom wasn't always the best gift giver, aside from books. Most of her gifts were practical – occasional clothing or shoes – what she thought I needed, not what I wanted, but that plaque was perfect, I loved it. Some years later, before we moved to California, I came home to find Annie, the woman who cleaned for us once a month, waiting for me with a look of deep shame on her face. She'd dropped the plaque while she was cleaning, and it broke into three large pieces. The archaeologist in me was thrilled, and told her so, but she didn't believe me. Only when she came back the next month and saw how I'd glued it, glued him, back together again, just as a good archaeologist should, only then, upon seeing my delight when I showed the plaque to her, was she able to let go of her guilt and shame.

The plaque remained hanging in Mom's house, in the room that had been briefly mine some years before. That night, after she and Merl went to bed, scared and in emotional pain from what Dad was going through and from what had happened to me, in pain and yet also partially numb – I took the plaque off the shelf where it was standing, propped it up against some books of Greek mythology on the floor in the middle of my old room, and lit a candle in front of it. Then I turned to the god of healing and said – "Help. Please help me."

As I sat on the floor, feeling damaged and afraid, the light in the room began to change and suddenly, out from behind the plaque – a man appeared! He was bearded, looked nothing like the man in the plaque, but I knew that he was Aesculapius. With fierce tenderness he lay his hands on my face – and I felt energy pouring into me! Then he vanished and I sat on the floor filled with light and gratitude. When I woke up the next morning my face felt better, and slowly some movement began to come back to it.

○

A few days later I went back to see the doctor again and he was amazed. He said that from looking at the condition of my face the first time he was sure that I would not get better!

I took the plaque home with me and it's hung from its leather cord in every place that I've ever lived in since that time. I never saw Aesculapius again, and none of my calls to him to come and heal my father were answered. Dad did great after his surgery for about six months but then the tumor began to grow back, in a place where they couldn't operate on it. He died in 1980, two years after his initial diagnosis, two days after his fifty-seventh birthday, and I miss him to this day and wonder why some calls are answered and some just plain ain't. Is it our karma? Our fate? Our destiny? A series of accidents? A deep soul choice? Or all of the above.

What my guides and angels and God in Her/His/Its various aspects have told me again and again over the years is that being in a physical body is the best place for a human soul to learn. That we all enter into each incarnation freely, by choice, but that what happens to us in the course of a lifetime can vary, widely. Once I was shown the image of being embodied as like a soul going to an amusement park and riding different rides, some of which are fun – a merry-go-round playing joyful music – and some of which are terrifying – a heart-pounding roller-coaster. I understand the image, it makes sense to me, and whenever someone I love (or even hate, which is rare) is suffering, I can step back a bit and see things from a soul-visting-an-amusment-park perspective – but I still hate what's happening.

CHAPTER 32

When I Got Reorganized

IT'S 12:35 IN THE MORNING, and I just woke up a few minutes ago with the answer to a question I was mulling over as I fell asleep – "Did I leave anything out?" Yes. And wide awake, I know exactly what it was. Is.

Given how important dreams have been to me, it's interesting that in a book about the major transformative events of my life – none of them are dreams. I've had dreams of past lives, dreams of aliens, composite dreams, lucid dreams, flying dreams, impossible dreams – but none of them are major. And if I had a dream that woke me a little while ago, me who led dream groups for several years, I don't remember it.

Dreams are like stories, I've always liked stories, and there *is* a dream I'd like to tell you. I was in my late twenties, had been working with a Freudian therapist for several years, and was moving toward my last session when I came in with a dream. "I'm in labor, alone, in a cabin somewhere in Vermont or New Hampshire. The labor pains are so intense that I pass out, and when I wake up – the baby is lying between my legs. I lift him up, his umbilical cord still attached, with no idea of how he came out of me. And he looks down at me and I look up at him, with a profound sense of mutual recognition. And I wake up, amazed." I thought my therapist would be amazed too. He was fine with my gayness but his reply stunned me. "I didn't realize that you had such serious gender issues. This would not be a good time to terminate your treatment." Well, I did, and began to take classes at the Jung Society, which were wonderful.

Here's another dream. On the night of Monday June 13th, 1988, I dreamed that I became the new Oracle of the Fishes. In the dream I was both a fish and a man, walking on a rocky beach with an older woman who was also a fish, she the one who appointed me to be the new oracle. Ocean, and fishes, represent to me the unconscious and its inhabitants, and the dream seemed to be telling me that my job is to speak from that liquid fluid flowing place of unknowing – but owning that part of me has been difficult.

And now another one, that I had around the time that God first came to me as Him, which you'll hear about later. I don't live in my apartment. I live in a very tall lighthouse, and from the top – I can see the entire world and see the rest of my unfolding life, and it feels right, good, purposeful.

But here is the story that I woke up knowing I wanted to tell you! On the morning of March 24th 1988 I woke up in my bed in Park Slope, Brooklyn. The room was glowing with morning light as I rose up into wakefulness on my back, not looking at the mantelpiece across from me, or the fireplace beneath it with my little meditation altar inside – on the morning of my 37th birthday! My head was on my pillow, and looking up at the ceiling above me I felt a gathering of energy around me and knew that until that very moment – I'd been living in the world, moving through the world – with my feet going forward but my head on backwards, always facing the past. And then, as I lay there, a tender, loving, wise, and powerful angelic force – very gently turned my head around, and for the first time in my life my head and my feet were facing the same direction, and for the first time in my life, instead of looking into the past – I was gazing out into the future!

And now, after writing and rewriting and looking at old notes in the lists of spiritual experiences I wrote some time ago, the clock on my laptop says that it's now 1:46. And I'm going to take a piss and get back in bed. Thinking two things:

One: My head may be facing forward, but this book is such a backwards glance.

Two: I turned 37 that day. In two days less than a month, on the 24th of March in the Gregorian year 2024 – I will turn 73!

○

It's now Monday the 16th of June in 2025 as I sit at my desk, rereading, tinkering, revising. And I realize that there is one more dream I want to share with you.

I woke on the morning of Friday January 3rd this year with what I called in my journal the second major dream of my life, the first one being the lighthouse dream I had in my twenties. In the dream I'm sitting outside on the ground with a circle of ten or twelve women. I'm a woman too, and we're all in our thirties, taking part in a past life trauma healing ritual. Several times I became lucid in the dream, wondering if I was there to heal my trauma when I was Josef and died in a gas chamber. Many of the women there I knew in this life and in past lives but I couldn't remember who they were when I woke up. At one point in the dream I picked up a worn alternate version of the book I co-authored, *Ask Your Angels*. Flipping through the book I found the text for the ritual that we were doing. Wow. I woke up feeling changed, healed, renewed, having looked forward in my lighthouse dream and backward in this one.

○

It was back in that time in my life, back in the 1980s, that a new disorder came into the world – AIDS. As a gay man, our community so deeply struck by an invisible presence, a virus that took so many many lives, I found myself called to join the New York Healing Circle, an amazing group of people, largely gay men, under the leadership of Samuel Kirschner and others. Inspired by the teachings of Louise Hay and by occasional visits from Ram Dass and other remarkable teachers, it was there that I slowly began to step out of the closet of my spiritual life and teach and lead weekly meditation groups. Did I tell anyone any of these stories? No! But with Samuel and my dear friend John Fletcher Harris, who left us so very long ago, and inspiring teachers like Nelson Bloncourt and Barbara Carrellas and Annie Sprinkle, who's still in my life, I found myself for the first time in a community of like-minded, like-souled people who became family.

Each Tuesday evening hundreds of us would gather in the gym of a Manhattan high school to sit, meditate, dance, sing, share what we were going through. On Thursday evenings I led a smaller group. And each week someone would share with us that Peter, Luis, Sunny, Tina, was in the hospital, back home, had died. Such tenderness and such devastating heartbreak, week after week after week, for years and years and years. To this day the New York Healing Circle remains one of the great blessings of my life. Looking back on that time, with Covid still in our midst, AIDS seems both less horrifying, and more, and with the growing homo/bi/trans phobia in this country and around the world, I am so grateful for the Healing Circle and the blessing it gave to all of us, that still ripples out in my life. And I hope that what it inspired is sprouting new branches and sending seeds out into the world. Truly a dream come true!

CHAPTER 33

A Reflecting Mirror

ONE DAY BACK IN 1979 when I was in LA visiting my ailing father, who was stretched out in bed in the hospital, he asked me something no one had ever asked me before: "Could you massage my feet?" I'd never gotten or given a massage of any kind, but I moved my chair from the side of his bed to the foot, took off his socks, and started to rub and press and move and then massage his feet. To my surprise and from his contented sighs, I knew that I was doing a good job. And the old and ancient me sat there contentedly, doing something familiar that I'd done before and always enjoyed in my other bodies.

Soon after that, back home, I was having lunch with my friend Ruth, who was in acupuncture school. I'd been feeling that much as I loved working in bookstores, it was time to find a way to make money where I could work less and write more. I said that I'd follow her to acupuncture school, but while getting stuck with needles never bothered me I couldn't imagine ever sticking one in someone else. Then I did something I've rarely ever done in this life. I asked Ruth to tell me what to do. She was silent for a while, sitting across from me at the table, then smiled and said, "You should go to massage school."

I'd always wanted to travel, not too long before I'd met someone who worked as a masseuse on a cruise ship, and even though I had never had a massage, I thanked my friend, went home, and applied to the Swedish Institute of Massage in Manhattan. It was a year-long program, I loved it, and it changed my life, both grounding and expanding me, enlivening me and giving me a whole new sense of direction.

My father died midway through my year at the Swedish Institute, but I did get to see him a few more times before that, and got to massage him again a few times before that. After he died, from a veterans' insurance policy he had, I received a check in the mail for what I still owed the school: $2500.00.

Back in those days most people still said "masseur" and "masseuse," but my classmates and I were calling ourselves "massage therapists." There were about thirty of us. One wanted to work in a gym, all the rest wanted to start their own private practice, but not me. Back when I was in junior high and remembering some old part of myself, I said to my mother, "I want to be a doctor," to which she replied, "You could never do that. You're scared of the sight of blood." So I didn't want to work in a gym or have my own practice. I wanted to work in a clinic or hospital. A neighbor of mine was a chiropractor and in the way that magic happens in my life, I ran into him one day after not having seen him for a while. We were catching each other up on our lives, I told him I was working on a new book, had gone to massage school, and he told me about his job and mentioned that his boss was looking for a massage therapist to work there.

I loved working in the clinic, and loved the dance I did between my mostly silent and fully embodied work days, and my creative nights at home – deep in words, in my head, and in my writing. When I was working on someone I got so very quiet that when it was time to ask them to turn over so that I could work on their other side, I would have to clear my throat and struggle to make words happen, while at home words would dance in my head for hours and hours and hours.

My office was in the renovated basement of an old Brooklyn mansion, and I was sitting in a chair after one patient left – today we would call them clients – when I could hear someone coming down the stairs. A moment later a lovely looking woman somewhat older than me, with curly locks of prematurely gray hair, was standing in the doorway. She smiled, I smiled back, she came in, I stood up and introduced myself. She handed me a clipboard and said that the doctor, my boss, had sent her down for me to work on her back.

Back? I read over the doctor's notes on the clipboard, then I looked her up and down, seeing both her energy field and her internal body, and did something I'd never done there before, and never did again – there. I said, "I see that your back needs working on, but what's really going on is an energy imbalance between the two sides of your body." I knew that in the way that I can feel all living beings vibrating, not hear them, as you may recall from an earlier story, but still feel them humming.

Barbara introduced herself, closed the door, sat down in the chair across from me and we had an amazing conversation about energy, unlike any that I'd ever had there before, and never had again. Until Barbara's visit, after talking about my treatment plan, I'd go out in the hall so that patients could get out of their clothing and into a hospital gown, and get under the sheets and towels on the table, so that I could massage them. But that's not what I did that day. I asked Barbara to get up on the table with her clothes on and lie down on her back, and then I began to do energy work on her.

Barbara got up from the table in a much more organized body, thanked me, said she'd come back the following week, and headed out. I saw a few more patients, signed out for the day, and headed to the subway stop, where Barbara was waiting too. She came up to me smiling and asked if I wanted to get a cup of tea. I told her I had a policy of not socializing with patients, which she was fine with, and we headed off on the platform to different places to wait for the train.

A few days later I ran into her out in the world. We chatted a bit and headed off in our separate ways. Barbara came to see me the following week, we had another good session, I saw a few more patients, and then went off to get the train – and she was waiting on the platform! I went up to her, smiled, said, "Rules are meant to be broken, and it seems like the universe wants us to know each other," and we went out for tea.

Soon after that we were sitting in her living room on the Upper West Side, having tea and eating something that I can't remember, and we looked at each other and the same thing happened to me that had happened with my mother – Barbara and I were in a different place, in a different shared incarnation. Looking around, we both agreed that we were in a very large elegant room somewhere, somewhere that we soon agreed was in Italy, Renaissance Italy. As we continued to explore our rearranged doubled-overlapping reality, we remembered that we had been sister and brother in a noble family, and were both writers and artists. Being very similar-looking siblings of a similar age, we also remembered, laughing, the nickname that everyone had for us – "the swans" – due to our height, slimness, and very long necks.

And that was the beginning of a friendship that began in the spring of 1983 and lasted for eighteen years until she died.

○

Barbara and I became what we called "dream partners," something that I've never experienced with anyone else and haven't again. We weren't always in each other's dreams. But far more often when I'd call her in the morning or she'd call me to tell me that she had a dream in which she was standing in line waiting for a movie – that was exactly what I'd been dreaming about that night. Or walking on the moon. Or flying over a beautiful beach – exactly what she'd been doing too in her sleep. And very often she'd call to tell me she had a dream – which was almost the same as the book I was reading. And then I'd call her a few days later to tell her about a dream that I had had – with the very same plot as the movie she'd seen the night before.

Over the years we led monthly dream groups and did some fascinating research about group dreaming. We put together two groups of people and invited them to dream together once a month and try to show up in each other's dreams – which they often did! We also wrote together and after I gave up doing body-work she and I worked as editorial consultants for Cheryl Woodruff, who you met before, and who is still a dear friend. (We just got off the phone a few minutes ago!) Cheryl was the editor of the book you've heard about already, here and in an alternate version, *Ask Your Angels*.

After Randy and I moved to California in 1994 Barbara and I would sometimes talk on the phone for three or four hours – a week! We continued to wander in and out of each other's dreams, pick up and start reading the same book without first talking about it, and be troubled by the world situation and wonder how the work we were doing could make a difference – something I still wonder about.

Benjamin my twin brother guided me here. Grandpa taught me to be present in the world. Nanny taught me about stories. Daddy and Mommy opened my eyes. Mrs. Winetsky opened me up to being a wordsmith. Erick opened wide the door for me to my spiritual life. Suzanne opened me up to owning what I do. And Barbara and I accompanied each other in our spiritual journeys for eighteen years – during which time we talked with angels, guides, with Goddess, past selves, including those on other planets, and we lovingly shared with others what we knew, what we remembered.

In one of our last conversations she told me she was going to reincarnate on a planet she'd lived on before, which she called Algemine Solis. She died on July 20th 2000, and from time to time I've gotten telepathic emails from there, where she's dancing, singing, and deepening her healing work. And it's only now that I see something I've never seen before – or ever thought about! That I began my spiritual journey in Santa Barbara when Erick opened me up to it– had my first major spiritual experience of opening up to all knowledge while standing by the shore of the lagoon, and grew to be fully grounded in this journey – from my wonderful amazing friendship with Barbara Grace Shor, of blessed memory – as we say in the Jewish world. Thank you Saint Barbara. I hope we get to meet again in bodies! Barbara, my best friend for eighteen years. In Hebrew every letter of the alphabet has a numerical value, and the letters of the word for life – chai – equal the number eighteen.

CHAPTER 34

My Second Blessing

OVER THE YEARS GUIDES and angels came and went. After meeting a woman at a party who could hear what everyone was thinking around her, who was about to move from Manhattan to a tiny little town in Upstate New York, I reached out to my crew and told them that they could never call me, that I had to call them first. We talked about it and worked out a deal that hasn't varied. New guides and angels can call me first, to let me know that they're standing at the doorway to my being conscious of them, but after they introduce themselves – I have to call them up myself to continue our conversation.

In the summer of 1985 an angel named Gantol came into my life and dictated a book on the subtle energy systems of the human body, which proved invaluable to me in my practice as a body-worker. At the core of it is a teaching about the awakening of a new major chakra in our body, the thymus chakra, I've been teaching classes about it for years, and you'll be reading about it soon. Gantol also introduced me to several other angels and on April 9th in 1987 my own guardian angel Sargolais revealed itself to me, in a much less dramatic fashion, and I realized that it/she/he was the being who'd appeared to me that night in my bedroom when I was a very little boy, and was the luminous being who came to me as The Grandmother when I was Josef. So I was writing and teaching angel work to individuals in my practice and giving workshops for gay men, using material I'd been channeling on the ancient roots of gay wisdom and culture.

On the 8th day of the 8th month in 1988 I went to a celebration in Central Park in Manhattan, where a friend, the Reverend Glenn of Trees, introduced me to his friend Timothy Wyllie. He and I spent the next few hours telling each other about our angel experiences, and a few days later he introduced me to his partner Alma Daniel, and we exchanged stories about our angelic adventures. While I had been sharing what I learned from the angels with people individually, the two of them were teaching angel groups and invited me to join them. That work led to our beginning to write a book called *Ask Your Angels*, solicited and edited by Cheryl Woodruff, although Timothy left Alma soon after, and while his name is on the cover, Alma and I wrote all of it but the prologue, which he wrote.

Around the same time a letter arrived in the mail from someone I didn't know: Raven Wolfdancer. He'd read a photocopy of my unpublished book for gay men called *Two Flutes Playing*. That letter led to others, then phone calls that went on for hours, which grew into a deep friendship with him – a gifted gardener, artist, healer, and visionary. Raven was one of the founders of GSV, the Gay Spirit Visions Conference, along with Ron Lambe and Peter Kendrick, and he invited me to speak at the first gathering, along with Harry Hay and Atlanta poet and therapist Franklin Abbott.

I was a shy fellow not yet forty, intimidated by the thought of speaking with Harry, co-founder of the Mattachine Society in 1950, the first sustained homosexual rights group in the United States, and co-founder of the Radical Faeries in 1970. But I said yes and traveled to Highlands, North Carolina to attend the first Celebrating Gay Spirit Visions Conference, which was held from November 2nd to 4th in 1990 at the Mountain Retreat Center. That gathering changed my life. I ended up going to GSV every year, spoke or presented at every conference, and was the only person to have a perfect attendance record for the first twenty years.

There were around 75 of us at that gathering in the lush green mountains. Harry spoke first, then I spoke, then Franklin. We ate together, danced, and had a very moving Heart Circle in which we shared with each other our deepest thoughts and feelings. Some of the men I met there have remained friends to this day and at the end of the conference Harry came up to me, put his hands on my shoulders and said, "I want to bless you as a younger elder of the tribe." Then he leaned forward and stuck his tongue in my mouth. Furious, I was about to push him away – when I saw pouring into his back a cone of bright yellow energy about twenty feet long, that filled his entire body and poured out of his tongue into my mouth, filling me from head to toe with that same bright yellow light.

○

Yellow. Both chicken-color, scared. And the color of the blanket the nurses wrapped me in when I was born, which you can read about in *Two Hearts Dancing*, the companion volume to my first gay book, *Two Flutes Playing*, with illustrations for it that Raven did before he was murdered in front of his house a few years later. And here I am, all these years later, no longer a younger elder, in my seventies as Harry was then, still doing my work and still feeling amusedly blessed by his blessing. (In fact last week I blessed someone for the first time myself as a younger elder. No tongue. Just my hands on her wise shoulders, spontaneously chanting a blessing for her.)

Harry and I continued to be in touch from that time on, and toward the end of his life he and his partner John Burnside lived a block away from me in San Francisco. I wasn't part of the amazing team of loving gay men who supported them as Harry moved toward death, but I would visit them from time to time and Harry and I always had long intense and engaging conversations about gayness and our sacred roles in the world. Another blessing!

CHAPTER 35

With Wings to Fly

SO MUCH HAS HAPPENED to me over the years that it's hard to believe. Past lives, spirit guides, the Creator coming to talk to me in my Brooklyn bedroom. Dead ancestors coming to visit and sometimes talk with me. Years ago I began to work with a succession of spirit guides, almost all of them gay, who taught me and dictated the information that's in my book *Two Flutes Playing*. One night during that time the Hindu guru Ramakrishna and his wife Sarada Devi showed up in my bedroom and walked into my body. Another time Sri Aurobindo and his consort, the French Sephardi Jewish Mirra Alfassa, called The Mother, did the same thing – showed up and walked into my body. Streams of past lives rose to the surface of my mind, as I wrote and worked, fell in and out of love, and watched the world changing around me.

Other than a note in my very first journal about the cosmic mother, which I began keeping in Houston Wood's class, it never occurred to me that God might be female. I had not yet read about people's experiences of Her in other times and places and Her coming was a rebirth for me. Whenever I turned inward, She was there with me and taught me many things. One was that there are a series of tiny fibers in my back (in all of our backs) that we can awaken, that become like wings when we unfold them. She had me work with mine till I was able to see and feel them very clearly, and if you want to learn more about them and open up your own, you can read about it in *Ask Your Angels*. She also invited me to open up to the energy of God the Father, which I resisted. My largely atheist upbringing and my connection with all of my lesbian feminist friends made doing that seem to be both patriarchal and life-negating.

All of that happened in Brooklyn, New York, not a place most people who aren't Hasidic Jews might think of as the ground for spiritual experiences, but for me Brooklyn was holy and I continued on there with my spiritual journey. On the night of June 15th in 1982 I was sitting on the floor in front of my meditation altar, which was inside the old non-working fireplace in my bedroom. The altar was composed of my great-grandmother's old brass Sabbath candlesticks that came from my great grandfather Alexander/Shabtai Two's Turkish Sephardi ancestors. I liked to rearrange what was around it – a picture of a winged Isis, a Hopi kachina, a statue of Krishna. On that night a black Buddha that I'd bought at the Tibetan Museum on Staten Island was sitting between those candlesticks. Actually it was green when I brought it home, but I didn't resonate with its greenness and painted it black with some shoe polish.

As I sat in my practice, which was simply watching my breath, I noticed a shimmering on the back wall of the fireplace. I remember turning my head from side to side to see if the reflection was from the candles. It wasn't. And I looked to the side to see if that shimmer was coming through the windows, but both shades were closed. As I sat there watching, the shimmer began to turn into a face, and then that face stepped out from the wall – turning into a seven-foot-tall, fully solid, three dimensional – (I couldn't even say the word to myself that night) – angel – floating three inches above the floor.

I was furious. My Buddhist meditation practice was about emptying your mind, not filling it with something else. And it was one thing to talk to spirit guides, even God the Mother – but angels, with wings!! I was furious – the angel went away – and I sat on the wooden floor thinking. "Why did I make it go away? That was the most loving being I've encountered since Nanny died," and decided that I'd rather be a bad Buddhist and see that angel than be a good one and live without it. That very instant – the angel returned! He had dark brown skin, golden hair, golden eyes, and enormous golden wings, and told me that his name was Gabriel. I didn't like that. Gabriel was a famous angel. His face was expressionless, but he was beaming out pure love to me, and invited me to open up my wing fibers. When I did, he touched the tips of his wings to mine and all of that love poured into me. My entire body began to vibrate, and I'd never felt such bliss.

Then Gabriel came closer, lay his hands on my shoulders, physically pressed me back onto the floor and floated on top of me, filling me with his loving energy, which was amazing. After a while, and I have no idea in clock-time how long that was, he rose up and vanished, leaving me lying on the floor in a state of utter amazement.

I remember sitting up very slowly, looking around the room and then saying out loud – "Oh my God. That was an acid flashback." Then I recalled the evening in my freshman year in college when I stood across from Norm and I remembered – that I'd never taken LSD!

○

The following night I sat down on the floor in my bedroom, across from my little altar, and Gabriel appeared again, less physical but utterly present, and floated over me again, and for the next few nights he came back again and again to teach me how to teach other people how to talk with their own angels. For the longest time I didn't tell anyone about his coming to be with me, and when I did start talking about his visit, it took me even longer to tell people what his name was. And I didn't mention the other angel who he sometimes brought with him, who had obsidian skin and whose name was Raphael.

Over time, as I got more and more used to being with angels, they stopped coming to me in a physical, visual way. They told me it takes a lot of work for them to show up for us in that way, that it's easier for them to connect with us through sound, which makes total sense to me, especially because the word for angel in Hebrew – *malach* – means "messenger." Once I got used to being with them I would hear different angels talking to me in different parts of my brain, which would light up when they were with me.

One night a few months later Raphael showed up in my bedroom in a visual way, again while I was sitting on the side of my bed, in the same place I'd been sitting when She first came to me. He looked just the way he had before, a tall obsidian-skinned man with wings. I was curious about angels and gender, and asked him if they're always, actually, male. As if I were watching a special effect in a movie, without disappearing, his body very slowly morphed from being male to being female. Today I might ask more questions about gender, but the world I lived in was much more binary back then, I understood what she was telling me, that angels are both female and male, and my next question to her was, "Do angels really look like people?" This time she melted down in a different way, turning into a six-foot golden sphere of light, and then in the midst of that light she extended herself horizontally into a seven-foot long golden dolphin with little shining wings, floating three feet above my bedroom floor. I understood what the dolphin was telling me, that they appear to each sentient being in its own form. But I was curious and asked, "What do you really look like?" This time the dolphin melted back into the golden sphere, which gradually became transparent. While I could see it clearly before with my physical eyes, as male, female, and dolphin, as the sphere of light reassembled, I could only see it at the very edge of my visual senses. There was a core of light in the center of the sphere, about a foot in diameter, with many long undulating fibers extending out from it, out beyond the edge of the sphere, pulsing in different colors and giving off a warm golden light. Sitting there in amazement, I knew that that was the closest I would ever get while embodied to know and see what an angel really looks like. And I thought back to my experience of dying as Josef and being met by an angel, The Grandmother, and going to heaven and then turning into a sphere of light myself, although I didn't have fibers of light extending out of a core the way that Raphael did.

Most people don't see angels. Once I asked Gabriel and Raphael why they came to me so clearly. Over the years, when I've taught angel workshops, I always tell attendees what Gabriel and Raphael said to me. Laughing, they replied, "It's because you were so dense that that was the only way that we could get through to you!" To which I always add, for the attendees, "If you've never had an angelic experience like mine, and if you don't see or feel your angel in a solid way in this workshop – consider that it's because you're not as dense as I was!" And down through the years they and other angels have continued to visit me, talk with me, and guide me.

○

I'm tinkering with this chapter, which I wrote several years ago, on the morning of June 16th 2025, the day after the forty-third anniversary of Gabriel first coming to visit me in Brooklyn. When I sat down to meditate last night – Gabriel was energetically sitting across from me, on the other side of my meditation altar. It – the angels' preferred pronoun, one of them recently told me, which I won't be changing in what I've already written – it, Gabriel, invited me to lie down on the floor facing north, as I had in 1982, and it floated above me, not in physical manifestation mode but energetically, and we had a short lovely conversation about my journey. What a blessing!

CHAPTER 36

Rising Higher and Higher

ON THE FIFTH NIGHT of his visits, the night of June 19th 1982, Gabriel once again reached out his wings toward mine, sending that subtle current through my body. And again he floated on top of me. But when he told me that he was going to carry me aloft in his wings, I got scared and pulled back from the depths of our connection. He asked me if I wanted to try again, and we began from the start, with his wingtips touching mine until the vibrating began. That time I was able to stay present, let go of my fears, and allow myself to feel our connection, through the power of his wings, a feeling both sacred and sensual. He lifted me up in his arms and wings and we ascended, through the high ceiling above me, through the apartment above mine, through the roof, soaring above the building, above the street, above Brooklyn, up over the Earth, in a journey not unlike but different from the one I'd gone on when I died as Josef.

Gabriel and I traveled higher and higher, through vertical court after courtyard, as if, in his arms, I was riding a cosmic elevator right up into the heavens. Each ascent and each level was more vivid and pure than the one before. I have no idea how many halls we rose through, but at last we came to a place that I knew was the final chamber that one could reach and still be conscious as a human being. It was a hall of light that was somehow both finite and infinite. It had floors and walls and ceiling, yet somehow went on forever. In the center of that hall was a throne, and on the throne was a being of light that I knew was God, God the Father. I tried to look at His face, but I was blinded by the light. When I asked Him what I should call Him, He answered with a version of the words that She had first spoken to me: "Call me anything you like. Call me God, or Allah, or Brahman, or Father, or El." Just as She had given me a name to call Her in our first encounter, Aphrodite, so too had He given me a name to call Him, El.

For years She had been inviting me to connect with Her Oneness by reaching out to Her Himness, but I always backed away. That night I was finally ready to open up to Him. He said, "Come closer." But I felt scared and sank back into my normal state of consciousness, back down to Brooklyn and my bedroom. Before I left I had a momentary flash of He in my right brain and She in my left. In that moment each of them was clear to me, then They merged, and a sudden thrust of energy carried me up and out of my brain, out into the endless light of the Absolute, whatever we call It: Tao, Brahman, Ain Sof.

Alone, I sat by myself on the floor, still tingling. I felt alive in every cell of my body, in touch with who I am and why I was born, conscious of the holiness of life and the purpose of the universe – as an outflow of God's own joy. And I reflected back on the name that He had given me – El – the ancient Semitic name that is the root of one of God's names in the Bible – Elohim – which is a cognate to Allah in the Qur'an. El, as in Gabri-El, Rapha-El, and Micha-El.

The following night, the night of June 20th, I sat before my altar and deepened again, expecting Gabriel to be there, more looking forward to being with him than I was to be in the presence of God, but for the first time Gabriel did not appear, and I realized that he had been there to guide me and that I was now on my own. As I deepened in my meditation I found myself rising again, up through the halls till I reached the Divine Presence. That time I could see His face of light, as fluid as the sea. Or rather I should say that just as I heard Her speaking to me in many voices, I saw His many faces, and all the forms through which He has been known. I saw him as a man of every human race, as horned god, bull, lion, eagle, and not just Earth faces but faces from many different worlds, faces changing as I watched, affirming for me that He is One, in all of His different manifestations. And in knowing that, the vision ended and I found myself traveling back down again, filled with a sense of beauty and peace.

The next night I returned to His presence, a little more easily. And I was also a little more used to Him, comfortable with what was happening, and willing to accept the reality of there being a Him. But whereas I was hoping for a vision that would help me better understand the sameness and differences between Him and Her, when I returned to the hall I had a vision of His absoluteness that was as full and complete as my vision of Her had been – a paradox, two different experiences of the same total Oneness. His face that night was not a changing face. It was a single face of light, of beauty, a face unlike any face that I had ever seen before. A new face, a face of love and peace. A face we all need to think about, as so many of our writings about Him are of a God of judgment.

It was on that third night in His presence that He gave me the entire section of the unpublished book of dictations that I call *God-Waves,* a section called "The Words of El," in which He reminded me that my journey was not to settle into a relationship with Him but to leave Him and offer myself up to the Unknowable, which is exactly what She had said to me. After I wrote down all His words and came back to my bedroom, I wrote in my journal about what it was like to return to the voice that first came to me in 1971, in a wadi behind Hebrew University – a wonderful reunion! And when I told the man I was involved with at the time what was happening to me, his response, which I also recorded in my journal, was, "I admire what you're doing. And I also think you're crazy." That was what I feared in 1971, but in 1982 I did not. I was open to the experience, excited to be having it, having learned from my years of listening that I wasn't going mad – but slowly going sane!

○

In *The Words of El* God told me what Goddess had been hinting at all along, that the images of Them presented to me were assembled on my behalf, and that there is a greater Oneness beyond Them, one that I'd been calling the Tao, or Brahman, or Ain Sof, and what some of my guides and angels and then El Himself called "Ahanah," accented on the first syllable – *Ah*-hah-nah – the conceptual bridge for my understanding that He and She are One. But even after my encounters with God, with El, in which I felt only love, tenderness, and bliss flowing out from Him to me, I found myself still carrying the baggage of several thousand years of patriarchal history and my Jewish roots. After the intensity of those first few nights faded and I was no longer able to ascend through all those courts to His throne, I found it challenging to separate my experiences from those of the prophets and mystics of old. Contrarian that I am, I realized that I was more comfortable with God as She than I had been with Him and, ungrateful animal that I can be, I wished I'd had a different kind of experience. God was probably laughing at me, and a few nights later He sent me this dream, which I recorded in my journal.

There is nothing, nothing but water. It is eternal, and eternally night. Then, somehow, in the heart of the waters, a swirling starts to happen, a coming together of Form in the midst of the uncreated.

As the Form gathers itself into being, the waters begin to recede. And as the waters recede, He rises up from the heart of them, the One, the Lord of Light.

He rises in the midst of the remaining water. And I watch Him as He begins to dance, begins a spiral dance. As He dances, infinite beads of water spray off His back, arms, chest, head, and begin to swirl around Him, orbit around Him in a joyous dance. And the beads of water become the world of matter, the world of the senses. All light, all form, all life, spinning out from His dance.

He remains at the center, still spinning. Spinning till the beads begin to swirl back toward him again, washing down His body as He begins to merge back into the infinite again.

And the waters rise up, till once again darkness reigns, and waters eternal. Till again is born out from the midst of the waters...

That's when I woke up, from a dream of a male God of delight who I found as comforting as I had found Goddess to be, in those times when reaching out to Formlessness is too remote and impersonal for me. Ahanah is a word we can use to describe the Ultimate Reality, but we were created and placed in a physical universe, and the image of that dancing God, the bridge to the Great Mystery, still makes me smile.

CHAPTER 37

Turning Into Light

OVER THE YEARS I continued to write and teach, to fall in and out of love, and to ask myself what I was doing with my life. I continued to go to the Gay Spirit Visions Conference, and in around 1992 I met Randy who I'd be with for the longest I've been with anyone so far, who you've met already. He was living in Louisville, Kentucky and moved to Brooklyn to live with me in my little magical two-room apartment. Two mutual friends connected us, Joe and David, who knew that we both talked to angels – but didn't know that a new angel had recently begun to talk with both of us, the same angel!

I only realized a few years ago when I was reading through old journals that I left Berkeley on June 4th 1974 to visit Dad and Suzanne – and on June 4th 1994 Randy and I drove off from 863 Carroll Street in Brooklyn and slowly made our way out to California so that he, a marriage and family therapist, could begin a PhD program in transpersonal psychology. We settled in a lovely light-filled four-room, two-bedroom, two-bath apartment in Menlo Park, not far from his school, where we slowly began to build a new community.

Randy was studying, I was both writing and teaching and spending a lot of time in southern California with my mother, who had had a stroke in her 65th year and wasn't doing well. Each year Randy would go off to do a six-day fasting retreat, and in September of 1998, when he went off, I decided to do a silent at-home retreat, based on Jewish Buddhist teacher Sylvia Boorstein's book *Don't Just Do Something. Sit There.*

I closed all the blinds and curtains and covered over all the clocks, set up a meditation altar, and took out my favorite Buddhist books to read in small bits during my retreat. I began the first day dancing around the living room for a while, singing a made-up song/chant to Ahanah, then I went into my room, closed the door, sat on the floor in front of my altar and lit the candles. Then I bowed and thanked Ahanah for the time of my retreat and for having created me, and entered into the silence. I took breaks to eat, to dance some more, and went back to sitting. But the first night, when I flipped through my books, I had a very strong reaction in my beating heart and said out loud, "I am not a Buddhist. I'm Hindu." I put all the Buddhist books away and took out two that meant so much to me, the *Bhagavad-Gita* and the *Upanishads,* to read along the way. And that was my routine for the rest of the week – dancing, sitting, cooking simple meals, eating, dancing, reading, and sitting again.

Randy would be home the next day, and I continued my practice throughout the day, distracted by a deep pain I was feeling in and behind my nose. But, pain or not, I was ready to wrap up my retreat. That evening, when I sat down on the floor in front of my meditation altar, instead of feeling my physical heart, I was instructed by a being I couldn't identify to focus on my heart chakra instead. So I did. And in the center I could feel a small aqua presence, which I associated with and assumed to be Na'shan, a name the angels had given me for my soul, my essence. Slowly that aqua oval in the middle of my chest began to elongate, like the lava I liked to watch each night in the Lava Lite my brother gave me for my 40th birthday. It rose upward chakra by chakra, till it reached the top of the inside of my head, where it merged with my crown chakra, and then an interior fountain began to cascade down inside me of aqua light. I had the thought that it would fill me up with aqua, all of me, and I was disappointed when it slowed down and in fact stopped spraying.

It was then that I noticed – damn, my nose still hurts, as it had in my earlier sittings that day. Not the same way, though. It felt like a lifetime of stored pain. And I wanted the aqua light to go into it and heal it all at once – but it was fading.

Then somebody (Na'shan? An angel?) told me to lie on my back on the floor and not block the pain but just try and feel it. Be with it for now, not try to do anything about it. Just feel it and know it, know what's in me. I thought – "Oh great, a torture experience. But why go on a retreat if you don't suffer?" As I lay back on the floor my body got more and more rigid, more and more contorted. "All this is in me," I thought. I got even more rigid, more twisted. More and more like Mom after her stroke. And I realized that that was where I was headed if I didn't change things. Then the pain got about as bad as it seemed it could get, and a voice and golden presence suggested I get up and come and sit by the altar again. So I did. My altar was a wooden chest with a single Herkimer diamond on a slab of green stone, sitting between two lit candles in my ancestors' brass Sabbath candlesticks, the same ones I'd been looking at the night that Gabriel first came to me.

I felt myself. I felt Na'shan in and as me. And I felt the golden presence sitting across from me, seated on the opposite side of my wooden altar – on the other side of the wall – in our living room! Even with a wall between us, I could see him clearly. I sensed and then knew that it was the soul of a man who had been my guru in a past life in India. I sensed that he was ready to take up with me from where he'd left off teaching me what seemed like it was almost 100 years before. I bowed to him. He bowed to me. In the midst of the light I could see him as he'd appeared. Long hair, a large strange mustache, long face, not very dark skin. All the while my body was aching, my nose was half stone and throbbing, and I hoped he could help me heal.

I bowed to him, he bowed to me, and in the space between us there rose up a radiant diamond-bright sort of a sphere of light that was white and yet luminous of all colors. Then it faded. And he asked me to bow to him again, and I did, acknowledging him as The Golden Guru. Then he bowed to me as The Future Aqua Guru. And when we sat up, the same amazing light was in the space between us. Now larger, brighter. Then it faded. And I was aware that he was my teacher, that he had experienced the light of Brahman/Ahanah in himself. That what was in him was in me too. And that I could allow him to transmit what he knew to me, to mirror it for me. And I knew he would.

Again we bowed. Gold to Aqua. I must admit I felt inadequate as Aqua. But when he sat up and faced me and the radiant sphere of diamond light loomed up between us again, at waist level, he raised his hands palms up to me, I did the same, and between our hands the light rose up, even stronger. Then faded. And we bowed again. And I knew I was ready to end my retreat, and I was happy.

But again he bowed, I bowed, we raised hands, and this time as the light came up, vast and brilliant, he brought his hands to face level and I did the same. Now the light was between us, and he suggested that I use my hands to direct that now almost blinding light into the dark empty dead spot in the middle of my face, at the top of my nose and all around it. I had to play with my hands for a while until I figured out how to direct it inward.

When I did the light grew even more vast, more powerful. It was light and space and more than space. As I directed it into my body I could feel it enter into the stone-dark hole in my face, warming it and bringing light to it. Banishing the pain.

It was then that I noticed that my hands were (my best word) *dissolving* into the light, becoming somehow the same radiant light, and a kind of limitless unbounded space. The light was pouring into my face and it too was now light and vast, space and yet not limited by space. My hands (or what had been my hands) were now directly in front of my face (or what had just been my face.) I still had the shape and size I had before, but both my hands were now light, pure, unlimited spacious light. And I knew that in a moment, if I kept bringing my hands closer to my face, that they would pass right through it and be inside my head. I could feel my breath on them. And I was terrified. Pulled back, as I had once pulled back with Gabriel about ascending. And the light didn't go away, just faded. And I touched my face, comforted that it was still my old physical self. And I could sense the Golden Guru sitting across from me again. It was all pretty amazing. And I was ready to end it. But he asked me to enter into the presence of the light again, one last time. And I did.

He bowed to me. I bowed to him. He was radiant. Much less golden. I was radiant. Not aqua at all anymore. Just pure light. And when we sat up and faced each other, the light rose up between us even vaster. And he reminded me of my experience in Santa Barbara in 1970, of light coming into me from above. And he reminded me of when the Great Mother first came to me in 1977, and I felt that too, gold of Her entering me after the silver cone of Santa Barbara. And the light between us rose up even more strongly and brilliantly. And I thought "This is Ahanah. This between our hearts is the infinite absolute Creator of all that is." Because what I was seeing was somehow a sphere around three feet in diameter, and yet at the same time, utterly limitless, infinite. And I thought – "This is it. This is my experience."

In 1985 Gantol had told me that when I was older I would have a third major spiritual experience, the seal on my two earlier ones, and that after it I wouldn't have another one till I was dying, that my death experience would be my fourth and final major one. It was a subtle sense that I might be ready to have this experience that had impelled me to create this retreat for myself, although I hadn't expected anything to happen as the first two experiences had come to me without my doing anything to get them, and

I always assumed that the same thing would happen with the long awaited Number Three.

My experience. My nameless teacher raised his hands up. I raised mine. The sphere of diamond light was pulsing between us, moving from chest level to face level as we lifted our hands. Again I directed the light into my face. This time it poured into my face, into my entire body. And as it did, although the boundaries of my body remained the same, I became space, pure space. And this time – I pressed my two hands pouring out light – deep into the middle of what had once been my solid head. My two hands were inside my head (what would a witness have seen?) and I wasn't afraid.

I left my hands inside my head for about ten slow seconds and then I dropped them into my lap. I was completely filled with light. I was no longer aqua but diamond bright myself. I had shape and yet at the same time I was infinite, limitless, immortal. And I sat (for how long in world-time I'm not sure) knowing that this is Ahanah. This is what I am, made by, made of, made from. I am light and space, limitless, timeless. We all are. All that is, is this. Light. And for a time, as I sat there, everything in existence felt whole and one again, as it had before I learned to lie when I was little.

This is what I journeyed for. This realization. This experience.

○

I remember some time before when I told Deborah my therapist and a student of a wisdom school called Ridhwan about my experience in Santa Barbara and about the coming of the Great Mother, and how I'd been promised a third experience of Ahanah – and I was pissed at her when she said that what would happen would be an experience in my body. Which seemed so small. Not what I wanted. And then – it happened, just as she'd predicted!

When the experience faded I got up, ate, danced, checked my email for the first time since my retreat began, and then hours later sat down to write about it in my journal, finally ready to put what had happened into words.

Just like at the lagoon in Santa Barbara and in my bedroom in Brooklyn, after each experience I came back to being Andrew. And at the time Andrew even doubted (in typical Andrew fashion) that what happened *had* actually happened. And yet he didn't doubt. Didn't doubt that what others might call "an enlightenment experience," had actually happened, even if he himself has never called it that.

This is what I wrote in my journal that night, the night of Thursday the 16th of September in the Gregorian year 1998:

> *For who he is, man, mortal, is breathed by light, eternal light. And that light is in my cells now. The mind. Maybe there's more. Maybe I will do it again. But the light was enough. I knew I was done. I bowed to the light, thanked the light for having made me out of the body of Itself, bowed to my teacher, opened my eyes.*

> *radiant*
> *effulgent*
> *limitless*

Some years later one of my guides told me that my guru's name was Shanti, and that he came back to work with me because of the incompletion of our past shared life. We were living in North India and there was an invasion of our region, I think by the English, and much as I wanted to be on a spiritual journey, I also wanted to defend our homeland and our people and joined the resistance – and was killed. Many years later I was told that several people I've known in this life were fellow-students in Shanti's ashram, including Grandpa and my roommate and guide Erick. And to this day, when I sit down to meditate, or do whatever it is that I do – I start by lightly and lovingly massaging my body from toes to head, then I reexperience knowledge flowing into me as it did in Santa Barbara, then that disc of light that was the Great Mother's voice pouring into me, and then I turn into light again as Shanti guided me to do, not so completely that I can stick my solid hands into my solid head, but in a luminous way that fills me with universal light.

CHAPTER 38

My Third Blessing

OVER THE YEARS I'VE continued to talk with guides and angels and God-dess, and I've often imagined my father's observant family saying: "We're glad you believe in God. But She, really?" And my mother's atheist family saying: "If you have to believe in a God, She is a whole lot better than He!" – but when I've sat down with them in spirit they've reminded me that who they are after they died isn't who they were when they were alive, and that they all know there's a Oneness we all come from, a holy shining Oneness.

It's the 20th of February in 2024 as I'm sitting at my desk, typing. Rain was pounding down a little while ago, then the sun came out, and now it's gone again. Looking back on it, this isn't the journey I thought I was going to be going on in third grade when I, the school artist, upon hearing Edgar Allan Poe's poem "The Bells," went home and wrote my first poem, or the path I've been on since Suzanne guided me to own my writing.

My primary connection with God has largely continued to be with God She, but my life has gotten more and more Jewish since Randy and I broke up in 2000, not too long before Barbara died, and I moved to San Francisco a year later, to live with Jay who I've known since before my bar mitzvah. Back in those days he was very involved in the synagogue two blocks away, Congregation Sha'ar Zahav, which was founded in 1977 by three gay men from Orthodox families. At first I didn't connect to the services, but I did enjoy going to Torah Study, and Dev Noily, the leader, totally reconnected me to my Jewishness. When Dev went off to rabbinical school I took their place leading Torah study, for two and a half years.

Over the years I've also taught classes, given more than forty Shab-bat and High Holiday sermons, mentored thirty-one bat and bar, or as we say now in our increasingly non-binary community – "b'mitzvah" students – and I don't know how many adults who were writing and delivering sermons, and as we were creating our own *siddur,* prayer book, I led six writing classes and worked with a number of individual writers who were crafting new inclusive LGBTQ liturgy. A number of blessings and prayers of mine appear in that prayer book, and as most of my own writing is on Jewish subjects – I now know that experiences like mine are part of our tradition, which we can read about in the Bible and in Jewish mystical texts, but I didn't know that as a little boy.

About fifteen years ago a gay rabbi friend approached me and said, "If we were Orthodox you would have been ordained a rabbi a very long time ago." The friend went on to say that he'd spoken with two other rabbis who knew me and that they were ready to give me *smicha,* to ordain me. I was awed, amazed, delighted, but didn't say yes. Instead I told my friend that I wanted to go home and think about it.

That night as I mulled over the possibility of being ordained a rabbi I could imagine my paternal ancestors saying: "Your Hebrew is terrible and your Aramaic is worse," and my Communist ancestors saying: "So you're going to sign up with the enemy?!" And I thought about a friend in rabbinic school, studying endlessly, exhausted, deep in debt, and didn't feel right about letting three rabbis lay their hands on me and instantly turn me into one of them. So I went back to my friend and said, "Thank you. And no thank you." He smiled, surprised, then said, "Actually, you're more a maggid than a rabbi." A maggid, a storyteller in the Jewish tradition, a role that was popular in the past, faded, and is returning to our communities.

I shared that conversation with Camille Angel, who was the rabbi of Sha'ar Zahav at the time, and – she offered to ordain me! And I talked about it with Rabbi Dev, who had come back to the Bay Area after their ordination, and with Sheri Hostetler, the pastor of the Mennonite church that meets on Sunday in Sha'ar Zahav that I've also been very involved with.

On Saturday May 12th of 2011, after the Shabbat service was over, I was sitting in the sanctuary talking with Rabbi Dev about my ordination, which was scheduled for August, when Sheri and her son came up the stairs and into the room, carrying shopping bags. She would be turning 50 in a few days and there was going to be a party for her that evening. Her son went back down to help his dad bring more stuff up, and Sheri sat down on the other side of me. When Dev brought up the ordination, we three chatted about it for a minute or two, and then the two of them leaned forward in front of me, looked at each other, said, "Let's do it now!" and stood up.

I sat there stunned, as they pulled me to my feet. Dev stood in front of me and placed their hands on my head, and Sheri stepped to my side and put one hand over my heart and her other one on my back, behind it. And then, as if they were reading from a prepared script, the two of them said the exact same words, which none of us could remember later, and their energy began to pour into my body. I was standing there in a sphere of light that began to shine down into all of my cells, that very familiar room seemed utterly changed, both larger and lighter, and I was feeling so very very very much alive, present and alive. Smiling, all three of us, they ended by saying the same exact six words, the only ones that we could remember later – "And now you are a maggid."

A maggid. Ordained privately and spontaneously by a rabbi and a pastor, perhaps the first interfaith maggid in history! After they said those words they stepped back, the energy stopped flowing through my body, and a moment later Sheri's son and his dad came into the sanctuary, then a few other people, and everything in the room turned back to the way it was before they raised me to my feet. Except for me.

Sheri's birthday party was joyous, and that September, standing up on the bimah, Rabbi Angel put her hands on my head and blessed me publicly as a maggid, with everyone who was there that day touching me or touching someone who was touching me, just as we do with a loaf of challah after a Shabbat service.

○

Sometimes I regret my decision, imagining the impact of a letter I might write to a politician that I've signed "Rabbi Ramer." Almost no one knows what a maggid is, even most of my Jewish friends and family. Although when I explained to my family what a maggid is, and told them what had happened when Sheri and Dev gave me my third life blessing, they all said, "Of course!"

It's June of 2025 now. This May 12th was the thirteenth anniversary of my maggidic ordination – my bar mitzvah year! That day was also Wesak, a holiday in the Buddhist tradition, and also a full moon, called in the Native American tradition of certain people a Flower Moon. I started the day in a Zoom call with Hunter, one of my best friends, and feeling flowery myself, I danced through the day smiling and deeply grateful for all of my blessings.

The next day, to continue my celebration, I took myself out to lunch at an Ethiopian restaurant in Berkeley. Then I met for the first time with a new conversion mentee from my synagogue. Such a blessing! We talked for three hours!

If you'd like a copy of our amazing siddur, which 141 of us worked on, please visit https://shaarzahav.org/our-siddur/ .

CHAPTER 39

An Amazing Vision

I CONTINUED TO WRITE, I continued to teach, I continued to talk with and learn from my ancestors, guides, angels, and from God Her/Him/Itself. In 2016 I moved from San Francisco across the bay to Oakland, and found myself loving being here way more than I loved being in San Francisco, just as I'd loved living in Brooklyn so much more than I had when I lived in Manhattan. What Prospect Park in Brooklyn was for me, Lake Merritt is for me now. There are pelicans, egrets, herons, ducks, and geese, which illuminate my heart. And the trees, the light in the trees, with thousands of crows circling over them each evening at sundown, feed me the same way the food does at my three favorite restaurants – Indian: Khana Peena, Messob: Ethiopian, and Persian Nights, right across the street from the children's amusement park Fairyland. That Fairyland a spiral back to the one in Queens that I was born across the street from, and there's some Persian-Jewish DNA in me, from the ancestor I call Shabtai One.

Oakland. Home. Here. Where the next step in my journey happened.

In July of 2018 I was sitting on the living room floor meditating when a gigantic jigsaw puzzle appeared in front of me. It was made out of gold with darker veins of gold running through it, rather like marble, and I knew there was one piece in it for every person in the world. One piece was pushed forward and I was told – "Everyone alive now has a share in the transformation of human life upon this planet, and this is your contribution." The moment I heard those words I knew that what I've been taught and been teaching about the thymus chakra since the 1980s is the very heart of my contribution, that's grounded in a workshop called Embodied Evolution. What's yours?

I felt the seed of my thymus chakra from the first time Gantol told me about it, and taught me how to awaken it and teach others to awaken theirs. People would often laugh at me when I mentioned that we have an eighth major chakra, in our upper chest, and one student yelled at me that we only have seven! After my first book was published in 1987, *little pictures*, I was interviewed on a cable television show with Dr. Brugh Joy, who talked about his own amazing work as a healer and energy practitioner. After the show, when I asked him about the information I'd been getting on the thymus chakra, he affirmed it and told me that he calls it the mid-chest chakra, and that it's also called the high heart, secret heart, and witness area. If you go to his amazing book *Joy's Way* you can read about and see some beautiful drawings of it, and of several other chakras too!

While the heart chakra is concerned with our capacity for intimate, personal love, the thymus chakra's function is to facilitate our capacity for joyous global connection. It is, in essence, the chakra of world peace. When all of us have activated our thymus chakra we will move in the world in a joyous way, knowing in our bodies and not just in our minds that all of us are one. I was told that after the very first nuclear device was detonated on July 16, 1945, that our guides and angels said a version of – "Oy vay! This is a step in the wrong direction and a big mistake!" They met in council, decided that something needed to be done, and created and implanted the seed of the very first thymus chakras in all of humanity.

It takes between three and five years to fully activate this chakra, but once you start working with it, it will begin to awaken and start to function.

AWAKENING AND ACTIVATING YOUR THYMUS CHAKRA

Read through the directions slowly, step by step, or record the meditation so you can play it back to yourself. Give yourself ten or fifteen minutes to do it. You may want to do this practice in the morning, before you get out of bed, or you may prefer to do it at night, just before you go to bed. You can do it in the shower, and you can incorporate it into your regular spiritual practice. The more often you tune into this chakra throughout the day, the more quickly it will be activated.

- Get comfortable. Relax. Close your eyes. With the tips of your fingers locate the place in your upper chest where you can feel a pair of prominent ribs jut out on either side of your sternum, a little below the notch in your clavicle. Lightly rub this area on your sternum for a while and then rest your palms there.

- Bring your consciousness to that area. Turn inward until you find a small warm spot of light between an inch and half an inch inside your body. It may be only a pin-prick of light, easy to skip over, much smaller than your other chakras if you work with them, midway between your heart and throat chakras. This spot is the emergence point for your new chakra. As you turn inward you may sense it glowing in a color in the blue-green family, turquoise or aqua, as we all experience it differently.

- To further energize and awaken your new chakra you can try putting the back of your wrists on your upper chest, about four inches apart, with your palms and fingers parallel to each other, your fingers pointing away from your chest.

- Tune into your breath. As you inhale, draw energy up from what my guides taught me years ago to encounter as our ancestors did for millennia, as Father Earth, drawing his energy up through the bottoms of your feet, all the way up through to the top of your head. Let your body fill with Earth energy and when it is, breathe it into your awakening thymus chakra.

- Next, open up to the Goddess, to Mother Sky, and inhale Her energy down through the top of your head till it fills your body. Then inhale it into your thymus chakra. Feel that the tiny seed of glowing blue-green light there is being fed by both blue-sky and green-Earth energies. Feel your thymus chakra glowing a little bit more brightly now, vibrating, coming alive as you align with it.

- When the inner light of your thymus chakra is stronger, you can beam it out into the world. Place the backs of your hands on your chest, with your palms facing outward, and send this shining light of peace out into the energy web that connects us all. You can send it to cities and countries, to communities, and to world leaders, to any areas of the planet itself that are in need of healing. See the energy of your thymus chakra beaming out to everyone in the world, shining into their own softly glowing thymus chakras so that they begin to awaken too.

- Now as you inhale, feel that you can receive thymus chakra energy from others, from the luminous green-blue aqua grid we are creating, all around the planet. Sending out, taking in – all of us joining together in a whole new way!

- To close the meditation, rub your chest over your thymus chakra again. Feel it glowing. Now, exhale the energy of peace from your thymus chakra out the bottoms of your feet into the Earth, and up through the top of your head, out to the heavens, sending peace there as well. Then withdraw your senses from that area and focus on your breath and your body for a minute or two before you get up, lightly massaging yourself wherever you can reach, to help ground you and this energy in your body.

CONTINUING STEPS IN WORKING WITH YOUR THYMUS CHAKRA

As climate change increases, as divisions between groups and nations increase, you may feel powerless about making a difference in the world. But in a simple silent and invisible way you can help to heal the world by working with your newly awakening thymus chakra. At any time of the night or day, as your thymus chakra grows and expands, you can send out and take in energy to and from others – when you're out walking, when you're standing in line in the bank or in a store, when you're sitting on a bus or train or stopped in your car at a red light. You can do this as part of your meditation or prayer practice. Sending out this energy to others will help to strengthen all of our immune systems, for the thymus gland is a central part of that, and in the face of toxic fires and infections and other tragic consequences of what we've done to the world, awakening your thymus chakra and sharing its energy is part of how we can transform human life on Planet Earth and help to heal the world.

When I first started awakening my thymus chakra, I met very very few people who had awakened thymus chakras themselves. Over the years I've met more and more people who have awakened thymus chakras, most of them unconscious of what's glowing in their upper chest. And these days – I'm writing this section on June 16, 2025 – when I walk around Lake Merritt I see more and more babies with their thymus chakras glowing in their chests – little kids who seem to know me and make direct eye contact with me, in a way that only happened rarely in the past. Yes. They're sending better babies! Wiser souls! And this gives me hope. Deep hope. In this challenging time in our history!

CHAPTER 40

A Glorious Reunion

YOU KNOW THE STORY. I started out life as a twin, my brother and I floating side by side in our mother's womb. Sadly, he died around the beginning of our second trimester, and for my entire life I've felt his absence, always on my left. When I was little I called him Alexander, after Zayda, who brought me back here when I almost died. So we were Andrew and Alexander. But back in my twenties, when my mother told me that if he'd lived she would have called him Benjamin, that's what I started calling him.

On October 5th 2023 I was standing at the stove in my Oakland apartment, reheating a pot of lentil and sweet potato soup with a big metal spoon. When I cracked an egg over the pot – there were two egg yolks sitting on top of the soup. For a moment I thought I'd gone crazy, had Alzheimer's, and forgotten that I'd already cracked an egg into the pot – because I'd never seen or heard of an egg with two yolks before – and I've been cooking for myself and others since my father left home all those years ago.

So two bright yellow shiny egg yolks were sitting in a pot – and then all of a sudden – I felt Benjamin standing beside me – on my left! I started crying with joy. He told me to call him Ben, wrapped himself around me, held me, rocked me and told me "You're going to be okay!" Then he was gone, and I was glowing inside, feeling warm and comforted by him.

For the next few days I felt him and heard him with a clarity of presence that I've never experienced before with any other spirit visitor. He told me that we're old old friends who first lived together on another planet, that we migrated here together, and that as old friends we've taken turns being each other's temporary twin, escorting each other back to the world of embodiment and then departing before we were reborn, which I always

138

knew on a soul level but not on a body level. He told me that in his most famous past life he had been (I'm nervous to write this, but here goes...) – Joan of Arc! – and that I was her twin sister and escorted her back here and died beside her in the womb. And that in my most famous past life I had been the prophetess Huldah, mentioned in the Bible, and that he/she was my twin sister and died beside me in the womb. Hearing these stories was an amazing surprise, and opened doorways to memories and feelings that I hadn't been conscious of before.

I woke on the morning of October 10th from a dream in which Ben had come to visit me, something that has never happened to me before with any of my other spirit companions. In that dream he taught me a meditation practice I shared that weekend with a gay men's Heart Circle on Zoom, hosted by the Gay Spirit Vision Conference. It's heart-focused and Ben's equivalent of my core thymus work, which you can read in the Teaching section of my website.

It's 2025 as I sit writing. Ben continues to visit me, sometime sitting across from me when I meditate, or beside me on my right. Left – absence. Right – here. He told me that we've occasionally incarnated together, once as sisters in our second Earth incarnations in Africa, hundreds of thousands of years ago, and once in India about three thousand years ago. But, as he'd already told me, most of the time we've been each other's guides in coming back here, floating in the womb side by side, and then one of us departing when the other one is solidly embodied.

○

As I was finishing my revisions of this chapter, Ben came back, stood behind me, his right hand on my right shoulder, and reminded me of something that I've been told before – that in most of what they call "probability strands," the field of unfolding possibilities, that this will be my last incarnation, and that after spending time in what he calls "rehab," reviewing this life and doing any healing that I need to do around it, that I will join him in his work as a spirit guide. And then a few days later he came back again to tell me something that I've sensed for some time but wasn't ready to hear yet, wasn't embodied enough to hear yet – that in the Native American past life twenty-five hundred years ago when I was Talking Deer – he was my lover Blue Hand, who first came to me in 1985 and then again in 2001, to dictate the information to me on our teacher Crow Medicine. Ben/Blue Hand. He also told me something he'd said before, that that was his last incarnation, and that he's been working as a spirit guide ever since. And here I am, living right where he and I lived all those many years ago, in what I like to call The Land of Oaks. What a blessing. Which gives me hope for my own unfolding future! Thank you for visiting, Brother, and thank you for sharing this with me!

○

Since the summer of 2017 I've lost more than sixty relatives and friends to Covid, cancer, accidents, suicide, heart attacks. There were months when I was so deep in grief that I couldn't take anything in, couldn't read, listen to music, or even watch a five minute video. I mentioned this to a friend one day who said, "I thought that you of all people wouldn't have this reaction!" And I responded, "I hear what you're saying. But believing in the immortality of the soul, that we choose each incarnation, and that I have conversations with and visits from the dead, which most other people don't have – does nothing for my grieving body! That I'll never hug, smile, talk with, walk with, share a meal, a story, with someone I know and love – is devastating for this embodied soul!"

I woke to an email recently telling me someone I know had died in her sleep – at age thirty-six. And I sat where I'm sitting now, at my computer, and I screamed at God for taking her and not this cranky old man. And I woke at 4:46 this morning and realized that I wanted to add this to my spiraling tales. My ouching.

A Pathway Back to the World

MY FATHER DIED IN 1980, two days after his fifty-seventh birthday. I had my fifty-seventh birthday party three days after mine, in 2008. I'm seventy-four now, the age my mother was when she died, in 1999, and I keep wondering – "Is this my last year? Is this my last book?" If it is, what a wonderful way to wrap things up, so that I can move on.

○

As you probably know, one third of the world's trees are threatened with extinction. There are half as many animals living in the wild today as there were in 1970. Climate scientists tell us that someone born today will experience three times as many floods and droughts and seven times as many heat waves as someone who was born in 1950, and they estimate that by the year 2050 there will be one billion climate refugees, escaping from heat, rising waters, droughts, and food shortages. Hearing this numbs some of us. Others wrap themselves in garments of denial. But my hope, in this challenging time, is that, as I heard wise elder Joanna Macy, who died this year, say to a group of us many many years ago: "What we're living through is the birth pangs of a new era."

○

On December 8, 2023, my brother Richard's seventieth birthday, when I sat down to meditate I felt a shift in the energy around me. Instead of my companion angel Sargolais, who's usually sitting across from me or is sphered around me, I felt a dark blue shining presence, a few feet in front of me. In the days to come he became more clear and said his name is Zadkiel, an angel I never heard of before, till I looked him up in my angel dictionary. Zadkiel says "Hi" and invites you to start to tell your own story, because:

In most of the probability-strands that we angels can detect, life on Planet Earth is going to get much more challenging before you all learn to connect and work collectively to heal it. And the world is going to need the innate wisdom you brought with you when you chose to incarnate again this time.

So sit, dear reader, breathe, ground, connect, open. And know that you are loved. You are wanted. You are needed. You are wise. You are ancient. You are timeless. You have both your ancestral and your incarnational wisdom within you. And you are not alone. Ever. You have guides. You have angels. You have God. So tenderly touch yourself, breathe, and know that you chose to come back into the world to make a difference! Even if you don't believe in the existence of the soul. Or believe in God.

○

A few weeks after Zadkiel first appeared, when I sat down to meditate, for the first time since I almost died as a little boy – I felt the presence of Zayda, my great grandfather! I couldn't see him as clearly and solidly as I'd seen Nanny and Grandpa when they came to visit me after they died, but I saw him as I did after I died when I was three and he came to bring me back to my body and to the world. He said he was only here for a quick visit and would come again soon. Then he was gone!

A few days later when I was getting ready to meditate, I felt his loving presence again. He said that he was very proud of me and came to visit because I'm in the last chapter of my life, and because he's getting ready to reincarnate again as a child with a Palestinian parent and an Israeli Jewish parent, so that he can do the work of reconciliation and healing that was so important to him when he was Alexander Gilman. Then he gave me a small implant – a little sphere of information that he placed in my third eye, to use in my unfolding journey. This happened to me once before, when one of my guides back in the 80s, Tayarti, a central figure in the first book of my trilogy for gay men, *Two Flutes Playing*, put an implant in my chest while I was walking in Prospect Park in Brooklyn. Thank you Tayarti! And thank you Zayda! He told me that I shared more past lives with Baba than anyone else in our family, and that my parents in this life came back as cousins in a biracial family in South Africa, a family of doctors and healers, which is the path that they intend to follow. And that Nanny is an older member of that family, part of a clan that I and all of us have deep karmic connections with.

After Zayda left, Lynne, Ellen, and Irene all came for a very brief visit. Thank you! They invite me to turn to you and ask:

> Who is reaching out to you right now, with love and information? What kind of wisdom do they want to share with you, your guides and your ancestors? And what can you use from this long spiraling story to support you in opening up to do the work that you came here to do – for yourself, your family, our species, and for all the world?

○

Angels, spirit guides, ancestors. During this period they guided me back to revisit scores of past lives, on other planets and here, in China, Japan, India, ancient Egypt, the Middle East, Africa, and the Americas, many shared with teachers, friends, and family in this life. And spiraled me back to my very first incarnation here, to a moment I've remembered for much of this life, a life in which, they told me, Lynne was my sister (we met in around 1975, instantly bonded, and called each other Sister and Brother) and Randy my former partner (with whom I'd moved back to California) was our little brother

In that memory, I'm a young man, naked and squatting on the ground, in a jungle in East Africa. There's a small stream flowing by, just out of sight, and light is shining down on me through the tall dense trees, like it did the day in this life when I had my first revelation, lying on the grass with Janie. As I squat there, I'm remembering my home world, from which I migrated here, with a stop along the way to incarnate once on a dying planet, in order to accompany some of its humanish souls here to Planet Earth, which had put out a cosmic call to come here to help evolve a landed form of sentient life to complement its sentient cetaceans. So I'm squatting on the ground, in a state of joy, awe, amazement, delight. "Wow," I'm thinking. "I'm here. In this glorious place. Yes. I made it!"

○

One morning in May of 2024, when I sat down to meditate, Shanti was sitting across from me, the guru from a past life who helped me to turn into light in 1998. Since that amazing experience I've never seen or felt or heard from him again – but he came back! To sit across from me, as he did all of those years ago, with a message for all of us:

On this beautiful endangered planet, you are needed, all of you who are Earth Healers – which is all of you who are embodied. There's all the time in the world to be dead when you're dead. Now that you're alive, be alive, be as fully present in your body as you can be, and deepen into and own and embody all the wisdom you brought into the physical world when you chose to embody again – for all of that work and wisdom is needed now, now more than ever in all of human history! And linked together from chakra to chakra, for the first time in all of human history, working together you can create the paradise that all of you, that all of *our* spiritual traditions have spoken of. Yes. Together. You. Us. Now. For all the world and all the living beings we share it with.

In the past year Shanti stopped visiting regularly. He told me I was more embodied in my humanness and ready to move on. One day Zadkiel told me that he was going to step back too, so that Uriel could step in, the angel, he told me, who created Sargolais and created my soul – fourteen million Earth-years ago – to incarnate with Ben and others on the landless planet where we sentients lived our lives in water. As I opened up to Uriel more deeply he told me that he was the old bearded man sitting on a bench in "heaven" who guided me back here after I died when I was little Josef. And then, after a few months of retuning, Uriel stepped back and Sargolais stepped forward again, a sweet reunion, rather like the one with Ben.

○

"What's in a name?" Shakespeare wrote in *Romeo and Juliet*. "That which we call a rose – By any other name would smell as sweet." I was named Andrew after Zayda, whose name was Alexander, and if I were a girl I would have been named Alison. My Hebrew name was Zayda's too, Shabtai, but none of my Hebrew school teachers ever called me by it, and I envied my brother Richard, whose Hebrew name is Ruven, wishing I had a Hebrew name with an A not an S sound.

Around the time of my bar mitzvah I read about Shabbetai Tzvi, a seventeenth century Ottoman mystic and rabbi – there are many different ways to spell that name in English – who said he could fly through the air, talk to God, claimed to be the messiah, and had a very large following in the Jewish world. But he was captured by the Ottoman authorities and given two choices by the sultan – convert to Islam, or die. He spent the rest of his life living publically as a Muslim but secretly practicing his Jewishness, and the Jewish community turned its back on him and has labeled him ever since as a sinner, a heretic, a false messiah. Learning about him, I went to the rabbi of our synagogue and asked if it was because of him that none of my teachers ever called me Shabtai. "Yes." When I complained to my parents and said they might as well have named me Jesus, they said they'd never heard of Shabbetai Tzvi, that they gave me Zayda's Hebrew name, which was also Baba's grandfather's. A name with a scary back-story, echoing into my own self-questioning. So you can probably understand why it's taken me so long to tell you this little tale.

Around twenty years ago I decided to change my Hebrew name, went to the library in my synagogue, Sha'ar Zahav in San Francisco, and sat down with a Hebrew name-book. Flipping through the A section, "Ayal" immediately caught my attention. It means deer or stag and I've loved deer for my entire life, even after that upsetting deer experience with my father.

The first time I had a meeting there with Rabbi Angel, who knew about my non-Zionist feelings, when she asked what my Hebrew name is and I told her, she laughed and asked it I'd changed it to that. I told her about the two Shabtais, and a few years later, after I discovered the name Ayal – in an outdoor ceremony at our annual retreat, with everyone gathered around us, she renamed me Ayal. Several months later I realized, laughing out loud myself, that in trying to escape from Shabbetai Tzvi – which means "Shabbetai Deer/Gazelle" I had inverted it and become Ayal Shabtai, "Deer/Stag Shabtai." The root of Shabtai is Shabbat. Sabbath. Rest. The spelling of which I use to distinguish myself from Tzvi.

I never liked Andrew or my nickname, Andy. I tried to change it in junior high, not long after my bar mitzvah, with my cousin Sara, who didn't like her name either. Going from Leslie to Sara was one thing, Sara the great grandmother she was named after. I wasn't fierce about it the way Sara was, who hated being called "Les." But no one would call me Alexander. "Alex, maybe." And I was always sad that I wasn't given a middle name. At a meditation retreat at Alma's in around 1988 we had to ask our guardian angel for our soul's name. When I asked Alma about it a few years ago she remembered it the same way. That everyone else heard something like "Ashandawara" and "Namarani," but I heard "Andrew Elias Ramer." Elias was Grandpa's grandfather, and Ramer in Yiddish, Grandpa told me just before my bar mitzvah, means Roman. Our family, I learned, had lived in Italy since the days of the Second Temple, and Elias's father sent him to a yeshiva in Austria, where he stayed and was given his/our last name.

There's a line in Psalm 90: "The span of our life is seventy years, or given the strength, eighty years," and on March 24, 2021, my seventieth birthday, Mychal Copeland, the current rabbi at Sha'ar Zahav, did a name-change ceremony on Zoom to which I invited more than a hundred friends and relatives, and I became "Elias."

About a week later Lynne called and said, "After almost fifty years I can't call you Elias, but I can call you Eli. And you can call me Lynden." (Her middle name was Denise.) Almost all of my family and friends struggled with Elias too – but Eli caught on! My theory: Andrew has 2 syllables, Eli has 3 syllables, Elias has 3 – a harder brain shift. And being Eli meant even more to me after Lynne died in 2022. Lynne, with whom I was recently told I shared more past lives than anyone else in this life.

Most people, when they introduce themselves, say "Hi. I'm Anna." "Hi. I'm Zack." Before I changed it I always said, "Hi. My name is Andrew," putting a little distance between myself and that name, but now, when I introduce myself I say, "Hi. I'm Eli," feeling a unity of Self and sound that's different from but not unlike the unity I felt before I learned how to lie. So, Eli.

But – am I Eli Andrew Ramer, or Andrew Eli Ramer?" Curious to hear what others might think, I sent an email to twenty friends and relatives who with only one exception wrote back: "I like E-A-R better than A-E-R. You're a writer. A hearer. A mystic. A prophet." So I'm still legally Andrew Ramer and still publish under that name, but you can call me Eli – although I miss my initials being AR, and if I live to eighty I may change it again. Perhaps to Ayal, or Alison, or to Androcles, which Dad used to call me. What do you think? And, what are you called? What do you call yourself? Could changing your name help you step into your own sweet life's calling a bit more, as doing it is helping me?

○

Twice in my mid-twenties, back when I was living in Brooklyn, I had exactly the same dream, which lasted for around ten seconds. I'm in my eighties, lying in bed, near the end of my life, in a bedroom with white walls, white curtains, looking out from under a white bedspread, out through the window across from me, out into an apple orchard. Several students, in their twenties, are taking care of me. On the bed, on a plate to my left, is a cheesecake, one slice missing. To my right, a bowl of fruit. My students are having a quiet conversation as my soul leaves my body and I step into the wall behind the headboard. One of the students, sitting to my right, notices that my pulse has stopped, and panics. His panic spreads to everyone else, and I say to him, to them – "I thought I taught you better than this! Turn and look around. I'm standing in the wall right behind the bed!" Then I wake up.

A few months later I had the same dream again, only this time the walls, curtains, bedspread weren't white but a soft pretty mustard yellow. And when I was in my forties and leading two workshops for gay men in Germany, Randy and I were walking through an apple orchard near the retreat center we were staying in and I thought, "This looks like the one in my dream. But – little old Jewish me? In Germany?"

About a decade after those dreams, when I was still living in Brooklyn, I dreamed that I went to a beautiful tree-filled cemetery to visit my grave. The stone was enormous, a foot thick and as wide as a king-size headboard. There were no images on it, like the one I designed for Mom, of waves, and I was a bit disappointed. Carved into the stone was:

Andrew Ramer
March 24, 1951 – September 15, 2063

Reading it, totally amazed, I thought – "Wow! I must have accomplished something in this life." Wow! My one big reservation about changing my name was – "Maybe Eli Andrew Ramer won't live as long as Andrew Ramer!" But who knows. Maybe longer. And, after all – it was only a dream.

○

It's July 21st 2025 as I'm tinkering with this book. Looking out over the flat roof of the building next door, out to the Cathedral of Christ the Light, the tall buildings around it, some trees and a sliver of Lake Merritt off to the side, here in the city of Oakland. It's a bleak gray chilly morning – and I am filled with light.

And I dream. Wake. Eat. Pray with my legs. Read. Worry. Write. Mourn. Laugh. Teach. Talk. Walk by the lake and watch the birds, the light. Do my morning and evening practice. Send out thymus chakra energy. Sit with Sargolais, and Ben, then wander some more. And spiral back to the most important guidance I can share with you, that comes from what my amazing teachers have taught me over the years:

If you can only do one thing to change your life – massage yourself every day, tenderly and lovingly, from head to toe, wherever you can reach. And if you can't, imagine that an ancestor or an angel is massaging you, tenderly and lovingly.

If you can only do one thing to change how you live in the world – be outside as much as you are able, on foot, in your wheelchair, not listening to podcasts, music, or talking on the phone, noticing everything and everyone around you, and sending them thymus chakra energy.

If you can only do one thing to change the world – plant trees, billions of trees, native to each region. And when you're out in the world, tenderly touch every tree you pass and whisper to it, "I love you and I'm doing my best to help to heal our world."

○

It's now 11 AM on Sunday the 24th of August in 2025 as I sit typing. On Friday I reviewed these spiraling stories with Hunter, the spiritual teacher, editor, and friend who walked with me as I was telling them and helped me organize them. And while I thought that my storytelling was done, yesterday morning God lightly whispered in my ear as I was sleeping that I should bring the book up to date by adding one more little story, the story below, that I came to – from writing this book!

On the night of August 12th God, Ahanah, rededicated me as one of Its more than two hundred thousand living prophets, which It had first done on August 12th five years ago, but never told anyone about. Yes, there are a good number of us in the world right now! Then God placed a sphere of wisdom-light in my belly, taught me a new mantra to align with the sphere, and guided me to a new place in my daily meditation practice.

For years my meditation practice has alternated between four steps: massage and connect with myself, my ancestors and guides, my angels, and then with God – and a practice of three steps: connect with myself, the angels, and then God. But on August 12th when I sat down to meditate, Ahanah told me that I had arrived at a place where my practice will be very simple: massage myself, and then open up to It, to God/Ahanah. A simple two-step practice that, Ahanah told me, will carry me through to my death.

○

So I dream. Wake. Meditate. Eat. Pray with my legs. Read. Worry. Write. Mourn. Laugh. Teach. Talk. Walk by the lake and watch the birds, the trees, the light.

Thank you so much for walking with me. I hope that something in these odd little rambling tales will touch and illuminate something wonderful in you.

○

Now I'm going to step aside and let Ben wrap things up:

> Feel your breath.
> Feel your body.
> Look around you.
> Look within.
> You are an Earth Healer.
> You are needed.
>
> Take a slow breath.
> Ask yourself – "Who am I?"
> Ask yourself – "What did I bring with me into the world?"
> Ask yourself – "What does Goddess want me to do with it?"
> Then go out in the world – and do it!

not: The End …
but hopefully a threshold to:
A New Beginning

> I keep feeling that there isn't one poem being written by any one of us – or a book or anything like that. The whole life of us writing, the whole product I guess I mean, is one long poem – a community effort if you will. It's all the same poem. It doesn't belong to any one writer – it's God's poem perhaps. Or God's people's poem.   *Anne Sexton*

Acknowledgments

THIS BOOK EXISTS BECAUSE of the blessings of everyone you met in these tales. Thank you all, in and out of physical bodies!

For supporting my root chakra needs, from the cup of which this book was written, deep gratitude to the three of you who sustain me. You know who you are!

My life is blessed by all the family and friends who are my regular walking, talking, meal sharing, letter writing, telephone, Zoom, and email companions. You know who you are! Your love and support means so much to me, and meant so much to me as I was working on these stories. Thank you, thank you, thank you!

For the wise friend who walked with me as I was writing this book, the wise friend who helped me tie all the strands together when it was done, and the wonderful writer-friends who wrote blessing-words for it, I give deep thanks.

With big thanks to the relatives who took the pictures of me, and to the friend who collaged them onto the photograph of what I look out at from my desk.

I'm deeply grateful to my spiritual communities: Congregation Sha'ar, the First Mennonite Church of San Francisco, and the Gay Spirit Visions Conference.

With deep wide shining gratitude to everyone at Wipf and Stock who brought this little book of spiraling tales out in the world!

With gratitude to all of you who have walked through these stories with me, wishing you every blessing in your own unfolding journey as an embodied sage and global healer.

About the Author

ANDREW RAMER, WHO GOES BY THE NAME ELI, is a coauthor of the international bestseller *Ask Your Angels,* a book that has guided spiritual seekers worldwide for over three decades. He is also the author of *Angel Answers* and *Revelations for a New Millennium,* as well as several other channeled works that invite readers into deeper dialogue with the unseen.

An award-winning writer, Eli has given voice to both queer and Jewish spiritual traditions through books such as *Two Flutes Playing* (a Lambda Literary Award finalist), *Two Hearts Dancing, Our Tribe Chanting, Queering the Text, Torah Told Different,* and *Fragments of the Brooklyn Talmud.* In a recent book, *Ever After,* he reimagined the lives of eleven iconic Western writers, in ten queer stories.

Ordained as a maggid—a sacred storyteller in the Jewish tradition—he was born in Elmhurst, New York, across the street from an amusement park called Fairyland, and now lives in Oakland, California, up the street from another Fairyland.

For more about his work, visit andrewramer.com.

www.ingramcontent.com/pod-product-compliance
Lightning Source LLC
Chambersburg PA
CBHW071442090426
42737CB00011B/1750